WRITE

BOOK

REPORTS

F

HARRY TEITELBAUM
DEPARTMENT OF ENGLISH
HOFSTRA UNIVERSITY

ARCO

New York   London   Toronto
Sydney   Tokyo   Singapore

First Arco Edition

 ARCO

Simon & Schuster, Inc.
15 Columbus Circle
New York, NY 10023

Manufactured in the United States of America

  2   3   4   5   6   7   8   9   10

Library of Congress Cataloging-in-Publication Data

Teitelbaum, Harry.
   How to write book reports / Harry Teitelbaum.
      p.   cm.
   "Originally published by Monarch Press"—T.p. verso.
   Summary: An introduction to the techniques of writing book reports
and reviews, including how to read correctly, note taking, topic
limitation, outlining, sample introductions, checklists, and
suggested topics.
   ISBN 0-13-441403-9
   1. English language—Rhetoric.   2. Book reviewing.   3. Report
writing.   [1. Book reviewing.   2. Report writing.]   I. Title.
PE1478.T45   1989
808'.066028—dc19   88-37242
                                                                   CIP
                                                                    AC

TABLE OF CONTENTS

PREFACE

CHAPTER   PAGE

one   *WHY A BOOK REPORT?*   1

         Differences Between Reviews and Reports .   2

         What NOT To Do   3

         Rewards of Writing Reviews.   4

two   *WHAT IS A REVIEW?*   6

         The Essay – Its History.   6

         Types of Essays   7

         Characteristics of the Essay   9

         Literary Criticism 12

         Authoritative *vs.* Impressionistic Reviews . 13

three *QUALIFICATIONS OF THE REVIEWER* 15

         The Purpose and Function of Literature . . . 15

         Knowledge of the Art Form 16

         Student's Limited Knowledge 17

         Subjectivity *vs.* Objectivity 18

         Substantiation 19

four   *PREPARING TO WRITE THE REPORT* 21

Reading the Work To Be Reviewed 21

Taking Notes 25

Extrinsic Factors 28

Familiarity with Genre To Be Reviewed . . . 32

The Audience 32

Reading of Other Reviews 34

Purpose of the Review 34

Checklist 35

five   *ORGANIZING THE REPORT* 38

The Thesis and the Outline 38

Introduction 43

Sample Introductions 46

Development — the Body 51

The Conclusion 52

Checklist 53

six   *WRITING THE REPORT* 55

Writing the First Draft 55

Some Aspects of Style 57

Revising the First Draft 64

The Final Manuscript 65

Checklist 69

seven *REVIEWING THE DIFFERENT GENRES* . . . 71

The Novel 71

The Play 74

Biographies 77

Non-Fiction Works Other than Biographies . 78

Collections 80

Sample Reviews 81

APPENDIX 91

Suggestions for Book Report Topics 91

Copyreading Symbols 94

PREFACE

It seems it's not the reading that you mind so much; it's that report you have to submit to your teacher to prove that you have read the book that often makes the "outside reading" so annoying, especially since you aren't crazy about writing to begin with. Hopefully, this book will make the task less onerous.

Remember that outside reading can be, and should be, fun. Its primary purpose is not really to torture you or to keep you off the streets at night. The purpose of outside reading is to afford you the opportunity to do the kind of reading that you may always have meant to do but somehow never found time for. It should be stimulating, exciting, and educational, giving you the opportunity to broaden your horizons, to visit other lands, other cultures, other times. It should make you soar to new heights.

That's all well and true, you say, but what about those reports? They, too, should be fun and exciting. But you must get over the idea that you are writing to please the teacher or to fulfill a course requirement. Writing must have a purpose, communication. That is, you must have something to say and you must want to communicate that something to someone else in such a manner that it is easily understood by your audience. This book is geared to help you accomplish just that.

Here you will find *suggestions on how to write book reports and reviews; how to prepare yourself for writing the review; how to review different genres; how to organize your review;* and finally, *how to prepare the final manuscript.* Careful adherence to these suggestions should enable you to write some fairly good book reports.

You have just received the good word from your teacher: the report is due very shortly, so let's begin working together while your resolutions are still intact.

CHAPTER I

WHY A BOOK REPORT?

Before you decide to spend your hard-earned money on a movie, you no doubt first check your local newspaper to see what the movie reviewer had to say. Through your past experience you have learned that you can rely on his ratings — or, conceiveably, you have concluded that if he strongly recommends a film, that is the film you will avoid at all costs. *Either way, however, you are selective.* The same holds true for the book review. With time at a premium and confronted with a plethora of books (not to mention the high cost of books today), we have learned to let professional reviewers give us their reactions before we decide whether or not to read the book.

Ideally, then, the function of the reviewer is to let you know if it will be worth your while to read the book. Of course, the reviewer, in order for his judgments to have validity, must have certain qualifications (see Chapter III) much as the sports writer must know all there is to know about the sport he is reporting on. And often the astute reader will not make a decision about reading a book until he has read several reviews of the work, but the chances are that if you read a favorable review and it is a subject of interest to you, you will get the book and read it.

Don't let the formality of the term *book review* frighten you. By now you have "reviewed" many books for your friends. Think of the last time you told your buddy: "That teacher of mine picks the dumbest plays for us to read. Can you imagine anything as stupid as *Romeo and Juliet?* How does she expect us to believe that bull about a guy

1

who loves a girl so much he attends a party only so he can look at the other girls and realize how miserable he is because his girl doesn't want to bother with him, and then he spots this skinny, masked fourteen-year-old and falls so madly in love with her that in a few days he marries her secretly? And then when he thinks she's dead — just because he sees her laid out in the tomb — he kills himself. And not only that, that guy Shakespeare writes funny. It's almost impossible to understand him. Instead of saying, 'Why are you named Romeo?'; he says, 'O Romeo, Romeo, wherefore art thou Romeo?' "

Whether you realized it or not, you were giving a review of Shakespeare's play, a meager, superficial, impressionistic review, but a review all the same. Over the years, you have done the same with movies and plays you have seen, with records you have listened to, and with concerts you have attended. In other words, you have given your listener, and possibly even a reader or two, your impression of some work, which, if you substantiated your impression to his satisfaction, he accepted. Thus, you have fulfilled, to some degree at least, the ideal purpose of a review.

DIFFERENCES BETWEEN REVIEWS AND REPORTS: These two terms are so often used interchangeably that they may cause some confusion for you. In essence, a report on a book — or on any work of art, for that matter — is all inclusive. It could limit itself to a totally objective statement of facts: title, author, price, type size, publication facts, conditions under which the work was produced; or it could involve building a set of where most of the action takes place; or drawing pictures of the costumes, or answering a number of teacher-assigned questions. On the other extreme, it could involve the writing of a critical review.

The review is basically a statement of opinion about a piece of writing (or any other work of art, e.g., dance, sculpture, music) substantiated with specific facts and incidents from the work itself. Its primary purpose is to let the reader of the review know whether it would be worth his while to read the work under discussion. Since you assume that the reader of your review has not yet read the work under discussion, you will have to include some information about the content of the work. But never forget that the object of the review is the presentation of the reviewer's opinion.

In essence, then, all reviews are book reports but not all reports are reviews. Since it is the writing of reviews that often presents the greater difficulty, this book will focus on that particular type of report.

WHAT NOT TO DO: Before we can begin to discuss the review in greater detail and how you should go about preparing yourself for writing one, it would be wise perhaps to point out what you should *not* do.

First of all, don't look upon the reading assignment as some form of torture conceived by your teacher to keep you in a state of slavery. Reading, especially outside reading, should be fun. This assumes, of course, that you have given some careful consideration to your selection, that you have solicited the opinion of your friends as well as that of your teacher and/or the librarian before you settled down to read. Be certain that you do not choose a book which is beyond your reading capability — or below it. It would be rather foolish for you to read James Joyce's *Ulysses* if you're reading on the ninth grade level — as foolish as for someone on the twelfth grade level to read *The Bobbsey Twins and Their Schoolmates.*

Second of all, give yourself ample time to read. Don't wait until the weekend before the report is due to rush breathlessly into the library to look for the thinnest book with the largest type. Choose your book carefully and as soon as possible after the assignment has been made. Then set yourself a program of reading. Set a certain amount of time aside every day during which you will read, preferably not at bedtime when you are so exhausted that your eyes will close before you even complete a page. If it is at all possible, buy your own copy of the book so that you can read it *actively*; that is, underline interesting passages and make marginal notes as you read. If not, keep small slips of paper handy that you can insert between pages for later reference. And if the book is really good you will find that you won't be able to put it down anyway; page will lead to page and chapter to chapter.

Third of all be sure that you *do* read the *entire* book. Do not rely on the book jacket blurb or on the summary in *Masterplots*. Even were you to get away with it, you would still be the loser. Reading really does open new worlds for us and gives us the opportunity to have experiences — vicarious though they are — which we could otherwise never have. Above all else, do not plagiarize someone else's work for that is literary theft, completely and totally dishonest.

Fourth of all, do not, when writing the review, simply write a summary of the plot and then add a postscript that you did or did not like the book. This is not reviewing by a long shot.

And, last of all, do not look upon your review as something that will be read only by the teacher (and, after all, he reads all kinds of garbage). Think of your review as being read by all your classmates and possibly being printed in the school newspaper with your name prominently displayed as the writer. This should force you to do the best writing that you are capable of doing. Be proud of your opinions and of your writing.

REWARDS OF WRITING REVIEWS: If you follow some of the above suggestions, as well as those which will follow, you will discover that writing reviews can be extremely rewarding. Among other factors, it will sharpen your critical faculties; no longer will your observations be limited to "Gee, that was really a great book; it was really great.

I really liked it." *You will learn to analyze your tastes, your likes, and dislikes, and back up your statements of opinion with sound reasoning.* You will, in time, learn to stand on your own two "literary feet" and express your opinion and interpretations with force and logic. And, if you learn to write effectively, you will find that you can influence the opinion of others.

Remember, that your writing of reviews is not limited to the English classroom and to your high school years. If your plans include college, you will be given ample opportunity by your college instructors, in almost all courses, to write reviews of one kind or another. The business and professional world, too, requires critical writing as does the world of community affairs. And certainly there is the world of our friends throughout life where we share our opinions of the arts, sometimes orally and sometimes in writing. And the more clearly and coherently and logically we can express these opinions, the more will they be respected.

CHAPTER II

WHAT IS A REVIEW?

Before you begin writing book reviews, it might prove helpful for you to become familiar with the *genre* (the literary type) to which reviews belong. An awareness of the origin of this genre and a thorough understanding of its characteristics will enable you to organize your thoughts and express your ideas more effectively and coherently.

THE ESSAY — ITS HISTORY: Until the latter part of the sixteenth century, anything not written in verse was considered *prosaic* or very common. A quick look at British literature from *Beowulf* through the Shakespearean plays indicates that most aesthetic literature was in verse regardless of the genre. As a matter of fact, writers like Shakespeare effectively used prose very often to indicate the commonness of the speaker or of the subject matter being discussed. Other than that, prose was relegated to correspondence, legal writings, government edicts, and chronicles.

It was not until the sixteenth century that a French writer, Montaigne, feeling the need to express his thoughts on a variety of subjects, decided that such *attempts* (*essai* in French) could be best accomplished through short prose pieces. This form of writing appealed particularly to a well-known Englishman of the period, Sir Francis Bacon, who chose to imitate Montaigne's form. And so the *essay* was born.

Although Bacon's essays would have to be characterized as *formal*, reflective essays, the essayists who followed him in many ways modified and expanded the genre so that today it has probably become the most popular vehicle for the expression of one's ideas and opinions. All one need do is to look at the daily newspaper with its many columnists to realize how diverse and flexible the genre has become, from an Erma Bombeck of *Newsday* who deals humorously with the problems of daily family life to an Art Buchwald's satirical writings about politics, to the serious, thoughtful writings of the *New York Times* editorials. In essence, all of these essays can be categorized into two main groups: formal and informal.

Whether an essay is formal or informal does not depend so much on the subject matter as on the author's attitude towards the subject. The *informal essay* will utilize an informal tone, colloquial language, and will not avoid the use of contractions. The writer will always speak in the first person and take on the tone as if he were sitting in the den or on the back porch and having a friendly chat with his reader on some subject of mutual interest. The *formal essay*, on the other hand, is a more serious approach to a subject of great importance, at least insofar as the writer is concerned. The writer will utilize all the rules of formal writing — avoidance of all colloquial expressions and contractions, a formal tone, the third person point of view (although the use of the "I" is now permissible in formal writing), and a serious treatment of the subject. In essence, the formal essay says to the reader, "Sit down and listen because I have something very important to tell you."

TYPES OF ESSAYS: There are basically six types of essays: descriptive, editorial, personal, character sketch, critical, and reflective. Although each of these has its own unique characteristics, they are by no means mutually exclusive; for example, the essay which is primarily reflective could at the same time also be descriptive and editorial. Perhaps, it is best at this time to remind you that any kind of classification in literature is never absolute; there are always grey areas where one type meshes with another. In such cases it becomes the author's intent that determines the classification. But more about that later.

Let us now look at each of these types briefly. The *descriptive essay* permits the writer to deal with any subject whatsoever. It enables him, for example, to take as mundane a subject as shoes and attempt to show, based on his observations, how shoe styles are indicative of the wearers' personalities. Christopher Morley had done something like that in his essay "On Doors" wherein he discusses the effect doors have on our lives, that one can never tell what is behind any door and that, finally, there will be that door leading to death.

The *editorial essay* is no doubt the one with which you are most familiar for it appears daily in your newspaper. It may be descriptive in nature, but whereas the descriptive essay can deal with the idle musing of the writer, the editorial essay has a very distinctive function — to make known to the reader the opinion of the newspaper (and not necessarily that of the writer; hence, newspaper editorials generally are not signed) and in some way to affect the reader's opinion.

The *character sketch* permits the writer to take some facet of an individual's life and present it to his reader in such a way that the reader becomes very much aware of the author's attitude towards that type of person. The subject can be some very well-known current figure, some historical character (e.g., as in Kennedy's *Profiles in Courage*), or some unknown contemporary whose traits or personal dilemmas the author feels are symptomatic of the problems faced by the average citizen. Remember, though, that the character sketch is not a definitive biography; the author is very selective, choosing only some facet of the character's life.

The *personal essay* is similar to the character sketch except that it concerns itself solely with the writer. What he is saying to the reader is "I am I; let me tell you something about myself and my view of life." It reveals the personality of the writer. The personal essay can be something as light and frivolous as Patrick Campbell's "The Intrepid Airman" (wherein the author rather humorously discusses his fear of flying) and Jimmy Breslin's "The Sign in Jimmy Breslin's Front Yard" (the author's attitude toward suburban living) or a rather serious self-analysis as Eldridge Cleaver's "On Becoming" from *Soul on Ice* (wherein he discusses his becoming aware of self) and Henry David Thoreau's "Where I Lived and What I Lived For" from *Walden*.

Whereas all of the above essays can be treated either formally or informally, the *reflective essay* generally demands formal treatment, and it is serious in tone. It "reflects" the deep, intensive, careful thinking of the writer on some important topic affecting life, such as death, education, politics, or human nature. The appeal of the reflective essay is primarily to the intellect.

In the *critical essay* the essayist concerns himself with some aspects of the Arts — painting, music, sculpture, dance, movies, theatre, or literature. He may concern himself with a critical analysis of some older work, of the works of a single artist of the past, or of some artistic movement; or he may analyze and judge a current work of art. In all cases, his primary concern is to make his reader aware of what he, the essayist, thinks and/or feels about the work of art. When the work being analyzed is literature, the critical essay is called *literary criticism*. It is this type of essay that encompasses the book review, and, hence, our primary concern here. However, before we go into greater detail, it is important for you to become aware of the main characteristics of the essay.

CHARACTERISTICS OF THE ESSAY: Although there is really no such thing as an absolute, fool-proof checklist that can be used to classify any literary genre, most essays tend to have the following characteristics: prose, brevity, distinctive style, incomplete treatment, literary wholeness, and personal tone. Of these, *prose* is the one that requires the least discussion since it is a form of writing that you are most frequently exposed to on a daily basis. Although you may occasionally come across an essay in verse, most notably Alexander Pope's "Essay on Man" and "Essay on Criticism," it is now generally accepted that essays are written in prose form; that is, a means of written expression used in normal communication, devoid of rhyme, meter, and, to some extent, figurative language.

Brevity can also be defined rather readily. All it really means is that the essay should be short, but *short* is a relative term, and if we were to give a word limitation, that would only be an artificial limit which might imply for some that if the work exceeds that limit, it is no longer an essay. That, of course, would be rather foolish. Perhaps, Edgar Allen Poe's definition of brevity for the short story should be applied here as well: a work which can be read at a single sitting, generally not to exceed two hours. The essence here is that, unlike a book which one may read over a period of days, the essay needs to be read at one time without any interruptions. As a result, we often find that parts of books — chapters in biographies, for example — qualify as essays. Among these are such works as Lincoln Steffens' "I Get a Colt To Break In" from *The Autobiography of Lincoln Steffens,* and Eldridge Cleaver's "The Allegory of the Black Eunuchs" from *Soul on Ice.*

Closely related to the aspect of brevity is the characteristic of *incomplete treatment.* Since the essay by its very nature must be short, the writer is precluded from presenting an exhaustive study of his subject. The treatment is incomplete in that the writer will deal with only one aspect of a broad topic. In that sense, a reviewer of a book cannot discuss all phases of the work; he becomes selective and analyzes those characteristics which he feels are of particular significance. Incomplete treatment is really little more than effective topic limitation.

But incomplete treatment does not imply that the essay can be lacking unity; the essay must be a *literary whole*. It must have a beginning, a middle, and an end. It must have an effective, stimulating introduction which sets forth the thesis; a fully developed, coherent, substantiated development of the introduction; and a logical conclusion. The reader should never feel as if he were left hanging in midair or that the writer has not presented his argument or viewpoint fully.

Although *distinctive style* is a characteristic easily applicable to all genres, it is perhaps of greater significance in the essay. As readers, we should always be capable of recognizing the distinctive style of the writer even were his name not to appear on the page. It is a writer's unique way of expressing himself which permits us to identify his work readily. If you have ever read anything by Art Buchwald, for example, or Jimmy Breslin, or Martin Luther King, you will know what I mean. If not, think of what enables Rich Little to imitate various personalities so that you easily recognize them; it is their unique mannerisms and expressions.

As a young writer you may not as yet have developed your own distinctive style of writing (although your teacher may facetiously have told you many times that she can recognize your papers a mile away), but you will find that as you continue to read extensively, paying attention to *how* writers express themselves, and continue to write, you will in time develop your own style of writing.

Most important of all the characteristics is *personal tone*. This characteristic is what distinguishes the essay from the other genres, for it is in the essay that the author reveals himself, his viewpoints, his feelings, his attitudes, his thoughts, his prejudices to the reader. In essence, he is constantly telling his reader "This is what I think and

what I believe. Listen to me and to what I have to say."
He may do this whimsically or seriously; he may be formal
or informal. The "I" is always very apparent. After reading
the essay, you should feel that you know the writer personally, that he has become your friend. It is not important
whether you agree with his views, but it is very important
that you know his views.

These, then, are the basic characteristics of the essay.
But, as has been mentioned earlier, classification of literature according to genres and the setting up of distinctive
characteristics can never be absolute. You will find, for
example, a work like Heywood Broun's "The Fifty-first
Dragon" classified both as a short story and an essay.
Broun's delightful tale of a young man enrolled in knight
school has all the trademarks of a short story, yet if we
look upon it as an allegory primarily concerned with presenting the author's views about the importance of self-
reliance, it readily becomes an essay. The same holds true
in attempting to classify certain works as short stories or
novels, poetic prose or prose poetry. Therefore, let these
characteristics act as a guide for you rather than as a
checklist.

LITERARY CRITICISM: Our primary concern, of course,
is the book review, or literary criticism. In his critical writings, the critic can concern himself with any one or several of the following:[1]

1. *Impressions* — What are his reactions to the
work? Did he like it? Did it appeal to his emotions,
to his intellect, or to both?

2. *Analysis* — How did the author accomplish his
avowed objective? Was the style effective? Was the
genre appropriate for the subject matter? How effective was his diction? his character delineation? his

---

[1] The category headings are listed by S. Stephenson Smith, *The Craft of the Critic* (New York, 1931), p. 15.

choice of setting? Was the work too long or too short? How extensive was his knowledge of the subject matter?

3. *Interpretation* — What does the work mean? What is the author trying to tell us? Can the work be understood without relying on such extrinsic factors as the author's background?

4. *Orientation* — Where does the work fit within the history of literary development? How does it relate to other works written by the same author? to works on the same subject by other authors? to comparable works of different time periods?

5. *Valuation* — Does the work have some general value? some unique value? Is its appeal limited to any special group or would it appeal to most readers? Is its appeal limited in time or is it universal?

6. *Generalization* — What broad, general statements can be made about the work?

AUTHORITATIVE VS. IMPRESSIONISTIC REVIEWS: Literary criticism can be either authoritative or impressionistic. The kinds of reviews you will find in scholarly journals and in literary magazines will generally be authoritative. Here the writer is extremely well qualified by nature of his education, training, extensive reading, and scholarly background to discuss the work with great authority, comparable to Hank Aaron's analyzing the batting form of a player. Such a critic can readily cite other works, critical theories, and literary history to substantiate his views. Needless to say, this is not the kind of review that you will be expected to write.

You will be expected to write impressionistic reviews, honest reactions to the work you have read. That, of course, is not to say that your review can be superficial; any expression of taste must be substantiated with ample proof. *But your review should be an expression of your personal reaction bounded by your experience, your knowledge, and backed up by sound reasoning and logic.* Such reviews, when effectively organized, logically thought out, and cogently presented, are perfectly valid forms of literary criticism.

CHAPTER III

QUALIFICATIONS OF THE REVIEWER

Even though you will probably be writing impression-istic reviews, you must still meet certain basic qualifica-tions. For one, you must have some understanding about the function of literature and the purpose literature serves or should serve in society. For two, you should have some awareness of what motivates authors to write and what they hope to accomplish. For three, you should have a knowledge of the various genres (or, at least, the one which you are discussing) and the basic characteristics of the genre. And even more important, you must be fully aware of your own limitations — reading ability, breadth of ex-perience, critical judgments. If you lack these qualifica-tions, your reviews will have little validity for they will be little more than "gut reaction" statements of taste which cannot effectively be disputed. But taste which is not based on something substantial has little merit; it is akin to saying "I liked it because I liked it and you can't argue with me." And that is true, but that does not make your reaction any more valid than anyone else's. Why, then, should anyone waste his time reading your paper?

THE PURPOSE AND FUNCTION OF LITERATURE: To attempt to discuss the purpose and function of literature within the confines of this chapter would be rather pre-sumptuous; critics throughout the ages have written on that subject. Let it suffice to say, then, that the true writer, the artist, writes because he has something which he feels must be said, must be communicated to a reader, and he would rather write than eat. Communication is the key word here, and this implies a two-way process. If the writer wants to communicate his ideas and/or his feelings, there must be a reader he has in mind (thus, it becomes a valid criterion of criticism to determine how effective that communication process has been).

Once we accept the concept that communication is the object of literature, we can then proceed to the next step that literature will be either utilitarian or aesthetic; it will either have a very practical, useful purpose or it will appeal to the sense of beauty, to the emotions. This, of course, does not mean that any given work can not be both, but one of the two should be dominant. The primary function of utilitarian literature is to teach (e.g., an encyclopedia) and that of aesthetic literature is to move or to stir the emotions as well as the mind.

Thomas De Quincey, an English critic writing in 1848, made the distinction more effectively when he called the former "the literature of *knowledge*" and the latter "the literature of *power*." He then proceeds to explain that "...The function of the first is — to *teach;* the function of the second is — to *move:* the first is a rudder; the second, an oar or a sail. The first speaks to the *mere* discursive understanding; the second speaks ultimately, it may happen, to the higher understanding or reason, but always *through* affections of pleasure and sympathy." To be sure, we can always learn something from what we read — and the most pleasurable way is from the literature of power. But whether one believes — as many did at one time — that the primary function of literature is to teach or whether one believes that it is to give pleasure becomes significant only if one accepts the communication aspect of literature.

KNOWLEDGE OF THE ART FORM: Before anyone can hope to make any sort of intelligent judgment of a work of art, he must have some knowledge about the art form which he is judging; otherwise it becomes no more than a gut reaction. For example, someone can tell you that a certain painting appeals to his taste and that he would be delighted to hang it in his living room; yet to an art critic, well versed in the technique of oils, this painting may be the worst piece of garbage he has ever seen. Similarly, someone can tell you that he strongly dislikes certain kinds of rock-and-roll music because it upsets him physically; yet to a musician that music may well be an outstanding musical composition. The same holds true about other forms of artistic expression.

In literature, the writer has a rather extensive list from which to choose. Depending upon his skills and his preferences, he may decide that the most effective means of communicating his ideas is through the vehicle of the novel; someone else, dealing with the similar subject, may choose the play — or the poem, or the essay, or the short story. Each of these has different characteristics and, hence, requires different skills on the part of the author.

It becomes extremely important, then, for the reviewer to have some knowledge of the genre being reviewed; the more extensive the knowledge, the better; the more widely read the reviewer is within that genre, the better yet. Without such knowledge, it becomes rather difficult for you to make valid judgments and to be fair in those judgments. After all, it would be rather absurd for you to criticize the lack of a plot in reviewing an essay. If your knowledge of the genre you are reviewing is very limited, you should take some time out to familiarize yourself with that form (by reading some critical essays) before you proceed with your review. Needless to say, the more authoritative the review, the more extensive and intensive one's knowledge should be.

STUDENT'S LIMITED KNOWLEDGE: This is extremely important. Nothing sounds as foolish as a statement concerning the universal worth of a book made by a student whose reading has been very limited. You cannot say that *The Adventures of Huckleberry Finn* is the best novel that has ever been written unless you have read most of the novels ever written. You cannot even say that it is Mark Twain's best work unless you have read all of Twain's works. The best you can do is compare *Huck Finn* to some other book with which you are familiar or, perhaps, state that it is the best book which *you* have read to date. Judgments which are not based on your experience and background should be adequately substantiated with proper documentation.

Be fully aware of what your limitations are and base your judgments accordingly. *Remember that at your stage of educational development you are not expected to be all knowing. An honest acknowledgment as to your limited knowledge in any given area will be respected. On the other hand, there are certain subjects of which your knowledge may well exceed that of your English teacher.* For example, if you are a ham radio operator, you can deal rather authoritatively with any book on that subject.

Do not be afraid, though, to make every effort to expand your knowledge in preparation for writing a review. If you are reviewing an historical novel dealing with the Crusades, why not read up on that period of history so that you may judge more accurately the writer's use of his background. If you know very little about Puritan New England, gain some background before reviewing *The Scarlet Letter*. Before criticizing Keats' poetry, you should learn something about Romanticism. And if you know little or nothing about symbolism and allegory, you cannot really review Hawthorne's short stories, for in the final analysis the reviewer should discuss how well the author has succeeded in achieving his purpose. And for this an understanding of the techniques of writing is essential.

SUBJECTIVITY VS. OBJECTIVITY: A good review should incorporate both a subjective and an objective view of the work. Although the impressionistic review is essentially a subjective reaction, if the review lacks any kind of objectivity, it lacks validity. As a reviewer you should be fair to the author, judging his work on how successfully he has attained his objective. For example, to criticize Albert Camus' *The Stranger* because the work lacks warmth, humor, and intensive human feelings and emotions would indicate an unawareness of Camus' theme. This is not to say that you cannot incorporate within the review your personal dislike for that kind of a theme or state that you feel that such a view of life is inaccurate, but you must maintain the perspective which permits you to judge the work with some objectivity.

The only thing worse than a totally subjective review is an objective review. Actually, an objective review is not a review at all; at best, it is a report, for the term *review* strongly implies — nay, demands — the reviewer's statement of opinion. A factual presentation of the conditions under which the book was written, a biography of the author, an accounting of books on a similar subject, a history of the genre, a reprint of the table of contents, a recounting of the difficulties experienced by the author in getting his work printed, a statement of the author's creative process, an accounting of the historical period during which the work is set, all of these would be totally objective reports, *but not reviews.*

Remember, then, that a good review is the proper blending of the subjective with the objective: the writer's opinion of the work, his critical judgment substantiated with details from and about the book, the factual density which lends credence to the review. The review should never be only one or the other.

SUBSTANTIATION: As you no doubt may well have discovered by now through your daily associations, any expression of opinion — or taste — not backed up with facts or sound reasoning is not very acceptable, nor should it be. It matters not whether the subject is outstanding pitching, good teachers, new rock groups, car performance, or television programs. You want more than someone's statement that "that's a great little car." You want to know why; you want proof. This is substantiation. Telling someone that *M*A*S*H* was the greatest movie you've ever seen is not very convincing unless you can also tell him why. In having to answer your friend's persistent question, "But what about it did you *really* like?" you may discover that it wasn't the movie at all which you liked; it may have been your date which made the film seem so enjoyable, or Elliot Gould — you love Elliot Gould and hence you love anything in which he appears — or you liked the movie because it was anti-establishment. On the other hand, when pressed further by your friend, you may cite the excellent acting in specific scenes, the camera angles, the cinematography, the humor of the football scene as substantiation for your statement of taste. This is substantiation.

The same holds true in reviewing literature. Reviewing demands a careful thinking and analysis of the work under discussion; it demands that you keep asking yourself *why* you reacted the way you did; it demands that you present ample proof to your reader to substantiate your views. This does not mean that your reader will automatically agree with you, but at least he will know on what you based your judgment. It is the substantiation, the citing of specific details and incidents from the work, which lends credence to your impressions and judgments.

CHAPTER IV

PREPARING TO WRITE THE REPORT

Now that you hopefully have some understanding and awareness of what constitutes a book review and what qualifications you will need as a reviewer, you are ready for the next step: preparation for the writing. This does not mean that you sit down and jot down whatever comes to mind, making your first draft your last draft. The emphasis here is on *preparation,* on the getting ready to write. Remember, no one ever said that good writing is easy. It is hard, time-consuming work requiring preparation, organization, writing, revision, and re-writing. To paraphrase Thomas Edison, good writing is ten percent inspiration and ninety percent perspiration. But all that work will be well worthwhile in giving you a well-written, coherent review that will make sense to your reader.

READING THE WORK TO BE REVIEWED: It may sound foolish to say that you must begin by reading the book or other work to be reviewed, but you no doubt know several students who have written book reports on works which they have never read, and, in some cases on works which don't even exist. If you do that, you're only fooling yourself, besides being dishonest. Do not read the book jacket blurb or summaries of the book; if possible, even avoid the commentaries of others. You will want to form your own unbiased opinion of the book. The opinions of others can be very misleading and cause you to expect too much — or too little. How many times have you heard a movie praised so highly that you were disappointed when you finally saw it although the film was really quite good? Your expectations had been too high. The reverse is also true. Begin your reading wth an open mind; that's the only way that you can be fair to the author.

First of all, schedule your reading for times when you are reasonably fresh and alert. Do not read late at night when you find it difficult to keep your eyes open. After a long day, even the most fascinating, exciting book will make you drowsy, and although your statement that the book put you to sleep will be accurate, it is hardly fair to the author. Furthermore, read sitting up in a chair with sufficient light behind you. Also try to read in an area where there will be few, if any, disturbances. In other words, *give the author a fighting chance.*

There are two parts of the work you should consider carefully before getting into the main part of the book: the title and the preface. The title is an important and integral part of the work. Read it carefully, and then think about it at some length. What does the title suggest? Is it a clear, concise statement of the theme or content? Is it symbolic? Is it an allusion? For example, what does the title of Lamb's essay "Dissertation on Roast Pig" suggest to you? If you expect a scholarly, reflective essay, you've missed Lamb's satire, for although the word *dissertation* is used for a formal, scholarly research paper, it is not a word associated with the subject of roast pig. You should, therefore, expect a satire on dissertations. On the other hand, Emerson's essay "Self-Reliance" is a very direct statement of the essay's content. If the title is an allusion, such as Faulkner's *The Sound and the Fury,* you should know that Faulkner is alluding to Macbeth's soliloquy, "Tomorrow, and tomorrow, and tomorrow" wherein he states that life is comparable to a tale told by an idiot, "...full of sound and fury, signifying nothing." Such a title strongly suggests Faulkner's theme. Once you have given careful thought to the title, jot down your reaction and put it aside. Your judgment as to whether the title is apropos must wait until after you have finished reading the work.

The preface, when there is one (novels generally do not have one), is also very significant. It is in the preface that the author states his aims and purpose in writing the book, as well as his limitations. It is extremely important for you to know the author's purpose for you are to judge the work as to how effectively he achieved these aims. To overlook the preface or to disregard it is a disservice to the author. Read the preface carefully, then, and keep in mind its main points as you read the work. *This will give you a very effective yardstick by which to measure the author's success.*

Not to be overlooked is the table of contents. Whether the book is non-fiction, or a biography, or a collection of shorter selections, the table of contents will permit you to see at a glance the basic organization of the work as a whole. If nothing else, it will let you know what to expect. Here again look at it carefully, especially the main headings.

Now that you have done all of the above, you are ready to begin your reading. But first be certain you know the genre that you are about to read, for each genre requires somewhat different skills as well as a different frame of mind. After all, you would not approach the reading of a history book in the same way that you would the reading of a novel. In the same way, reading lyrical poetry requires skills quite different from reading short stories.

Preferably, get your own copy of the book, one that you can read *actively*. The best way to read is with pencil in hand, underlining significant portions, making marginal notes, "questioning" statements made by the author or agreeing with him. If getting your own copy is not possible, keep small slips of paper on the side so that you can jot down your reactions as they occur. Insert these slips into the book for later reference. It is most important that you read the *entire* book, especially if the book is boring or badly written. It would be grossly unfair to make judgments based on either a part of a book or on a cursory reading. *Be prepared to read the work twice; the first time for a general impression, the second time for details and verification of that impression.* This is especially important when reading either technical material, poetry, or very symbolic works. Remember, be as thorough and perceptive in your reading as you possibly can so that you cannot be accused of having made judgments based on a superficial reading or on irrelevancies.

Here is a checklist you can use for your reading:

1. Avoid reading blurbs, summaries, and commentaries *prior* to the reading of the work.

2. Read only when you are fresh and alert.

3. Read with proper lighting and with a minimum of disturbances and interruptions.

4. Give careful thought to the title of the work and its significance and implication.

5. Read the preface to familiarize yourself with the author's intent.

6. Look over the table of contents (if there is one) so that you will be aware of the book's basic organization.

7. Know the genre to which the book belongs so that you may judge the work accordingly.

8. Get your own copy of the work, if possible, so that you can read actively.

9. If you use somebody else's book, keep slips of paper available for jotting down your reactions. Insert these slips within the book.

10. Read the *entire* book: get a general impression, and *think* about the work. Let it lie fallow in your mind until you see it in proper perspective.

11. Read the work again, this time for details to substantiate your initial impression or to modify that impression.

12. Be thorough and perceptive in your reading so that you can be fair to the author.

TAKING NOTES: No doubt, your normal pattern is to avoid taking notes at all costs, especially if you are reading aesthetic literature. After all, you argue, why destroy the pleasure of reading by stopping to jot down notes on paper; and, besides, you feel that your reaction to what you have just read is so firmly implanted in your mind that you will never forget it, certainly not within the next few days. But as experience has probably taught you by now, you know that this isn't true; that although you may recall that you had a reaction, by the time you finish reading the work you are no longer quite certain what that reaction was. The only logical solution, then, is to take notes. You will find that the time spent doing so will be well worthwhile in helping you to organize the review when the time comes to write.

Do not begin by taking copious notes on long sheets of paper. Rather, as has been suggested before, try to get a personal copy of the work so that you can underline and make marginal notes. If not, put in slips of paper to mark those pages that you want to refer to later. In this way, there will be a minimum of interference with your reading pleasure. But do keep that pencil by your side and *read actively, much as you would if you were involved in a direct discussion with the author.* Don't be passive: *react, agree, argue, debate, rebut!*

Here are some of the items that you should concern yourself with as you read:

1. *Point of view* — From what point of view is the work written? This is especially important in the realm of fiction writing. Does the writer write in the first person (referring to himself as "I")? Is the "I" of the work (the person) actually the writer speaking or is it a literary device where the "I" is one of the characters in the work? Would the work be more effective if we could see the story through the eyes of another character? Is the omniscient point of view used?

2. *Title and preface* — How accurate and effective is the title? Having read the work, do you feel that the title effectively created the tone and mood? Did the title become increasingly meaningful as you continued reading? Was the title mainly a means of capturing the reader's attention? Was it too broad or too narrow in scope? How much does the effectiveness of the title depend on the reader's outside knowledge? Does the title perhaps appeal to only one segment of the reading public and is it the same segment that the work is aimed at?

If the author stated his purpose in the preface, how effectively did he accomplish that purpose in the work? Did he adhere to his stated thesis? To what extent did he introduce tangential material? Is the reading of the preface necessary for an understanding of the work?

3. *Organization* — How well is the work organized? If fiction, is the story told chronologically or *in medias res* (beginning in the middle and relating events through a series of flashbacks as in Homer's *The Iliad*)? If non-fiction, does one chapter logically lead to the next? Is there ample substantiation? Are chapter titles clear and concise? If collections, how sound is the rationale for the selection of the shorter works? Are they logically organized? Is it necessary to read the selections in order? If so, is this a weakness in the organization?

4. *Style* — What style of writing does the author utilize? Is it formal or informal? Is it apropos to his subject and to the tone? What about his diction? Is it too difficult for the "average" reader? Does the style tend to appeal to only a select audience, for example, one ethinc group? How effective is the style in furthering the theme, that is, is *how* the author is saying it an aid or a hindrance to *what* he is saying? How much effort is required on the reader's part in comprehending the work (e.g., Joyce's stream-of-consciousness)?

5. *Theme* — What *is* the theme of the work? How readily apparent is that theme? How effectively does the

writer make the reader aware of the theme? Is it logically and/or cogently presented? If the work is fiction or poetry, how much symbolism does the writer employ and is the symbolism apparent to the astute reader? How convincing is the writer?

6. *The ending* — The ending of any work should be a logical outgrowth of what has been presented to that point. How effectively has the writer achieved that? Does the ending seem contrived, a *deus ex machina*? Does the work just sort of stop? Is the main character's conflict resolved satisfactorily, albeit not necessarily happily? Should the work have been ended before it did? After you have finished reading the work, how do you feel? Do you forget about it almost immediately or does it stay with you for a while? Were you able to guess the ending long before the end of the work?

7. *Accuracy of information* — Assuming you are qualified to make such judgments, how accurate was the information in the work? Were the facts distorted in any way? Were the author's prejudices apparent? Did he omit some significant events, thus affecting his accuracy? Does he document his sources? Are they reliable sources? In works of fiction, does he make ample use of factual density (supply enough facts to make the work credible)?

8. *Literary devices* What kinds of literary devices does the author employ, if any? Does he use symbolism? allusion? figurative language? Are the devices recognizable? Are they effective? If they seem obscure, could it be your inadequacy?

9. *Typography* — What about the layout of the book? Is the type too small? If pictures and/or illustrations and graphs are used, do they add anything to the work as a whole or are they simply there to fill out the book? Are the illustrations and graphs clear and readily understandable? Does the work contain an overabundance of footnotes? Are any textual notes clearly and concisely presented on

the same page or must one constantly turn to the back of the book? Is the overall layout attractive? How relevant is the book jacket to the book's content?

Of course, you will not be able to incorporate all of the foregoing into any one review, nor should you. But even though some of these items may not even be applicable to the work you are about to review, it is good to keep them in mind as you read. *Which of these you will use will depend on the work and on your reaction to the work.*

Once you determine which of these items you will utilize, look the book over again (better yet, re-read it) and begin marshalling the details, incidents, examples, quotations, paraphrases to help you substantiate your viewpoint. Choose your documentary evidence carefully. Avoid citing or quoting portions out of context so that the author's meaning is distorted. Do not focus on minute points. In quoting, quote accurately, and be sure to punctuate the quotation correctly; but do not over-quote. Avoid lengthy quoted passages.

At this point, do not be overly concerned with the relevance of your notes. *You should be taking many more notes than you will actually use in the writing of your report.* The main purpose at this time is to collect all information which might have some potential value for you and which will help you later on in formulating your thesis and in outlining your paper. Where possible, avoid taking notes on separate sheets of paper, but utilize the margins of your copy of the work. Or insert slips of paper which such pithy comments as "Quote from *Humble* to *language* in last para." or "good example of humor" or "ridiculous argument." Don't hesitate to use abbreviations since these notes are there only to serve as reminders to you.

EXTRINSIC FACTORS: One of the areas of critical controversy during this century has been to what extent extrinsic factors (factors *outside* of the work as opposed to intrinsic factors) should be employed in the critical analysis of literary works. There are those who staunchly maintain that any interpretation or analysis of a work must be based on the work itself and that references to material outside of the work may well color and affect the critic's evaluation. To these textual critics "...Biography is irrelevant; social background is irrelevant; nothing matters but the work of literature, and this the student scrutinizes with the care and precision of a microbiologist examining a segment of tissue."[1] On the other hand, there are the biographical-critical and historical-critical oriented critics who are convinced that bringing in from the outside "...all kinds of rich relevancies and connecting them with the poem..."[2] enriches the work, something which staying "inside the poem" will not permit. Valid arguments are presented by both sides and the tendency today is to take more of a middle-of-the-road approach. Your concern in reviewing a book (or anything else for that matter) should be that you do not use any extrinsic factors as a short cut to an understanding of the work or as a means of evaluating the work. It is best to hold off on familiarizing yourself with the extrinsic factors until *after* you have read the work and have come to some conclusions of your own. Then by all means gather all the background you can and see how, if at all, such background casts new light on the work.

Here are some of the extrinsic factors that may help you in better understanding and evaluating the work read:

1. *Biography* — Facets of the author's life can be helpful in more effectively evaluating his work. However, great care must be taken that you concern yourself only

---

[1]Granville Hicks, "Literary Horizons: Gestation of a Brain Child," *Saturday Review*, 45:62, January 6, 1962, citing W. M. Frohock, *Strangers to This Ground.*
[2]Leslie A Fiedler, "Archetype and Signature: A Study of the Relationship between Biography and Poetry," *Sewanee Review*, 40: 257, 1952.

with those portions of his life relevant to the work. For example, it might be very helpful to know that the author of a physics text is a well-known physicist and Nobel Prize winner, or that a science-fiction writer is also a scientist. On the other hand, knowing that Elizabeth Barrett Browning was deeply in love when she wrote her sonnets may be interesting but it should in no way affect the interpretation or evaluation of those very sonnets. Remember, do not present your reader with a full-length biography of the author or, worse, with a random collection of facts which have no bearing on the work. Select only those details which will enable your reader to become more convinced of the soundness of your judgment.

2. *Literary period* — The placement of a work in its literary period could be very helpful. This, of course, implies that you as a reviewer are familiar with at least the major aspects of that period. For example, to judge Wordsworth's works according to "classical" standards would be grossly unjust. You should know something about Romanticism in order to evaluate his works fairly. And, if necessary, you should make some of this knowledge available to your readers. Here, again, do not present a lengthy dissertation on all the aspects of the period; choose only those factors which are necessary for a clearer understanding of the work.

Since historical, political, and economic factors influence the writer (who, in turn, through his writings has a profound effect on them, e.g., the Abolitionists writing prior to the Civil War), you should have some awareness of the time period during which the author wrote. To understand Faulkner fully, for example, it is necessary to know something about life in the South during the early part of this century; in the same way, to understand Hemingway's *The Sun Also Rises,* one should know something about the Lost Generation of the 1920's and the events preceding that time period. Here again it may become necessary to give your reader some of this historical background.

3. *Author's intentions* — It is always helpful to the reviewer if he knows what the author's intentions were in writing the work since, in the final analysis, one of the main functions of the review is to determine how successful the author was in achieving his purpose. Clues to the author's intent can be derived from reading the preface, from interviews, and sometimes from contacting the author personally. However, the well-written work will readily reveal the author's intent.

4. *Author's qualifications* — Another factor which becomes a valid area for your concern as a reviewer is the author's qualifications to deal with the subject of his work. In the realm of non-fiction, this is of course rather apparent. For example, as qualified as the writer may be as a mathematician, he is not qualified to write authoritatively on genetics. In the realm of aesthetic literature it is another matter. Although personal experiences, the kind that Hemingway had and then wrote about, are the best source for writing, the author can prepare himself in other ways for dealing with his subject. Stephen Crane, for example, did not fight in the Civil War nor was he directly involved in combat, yet his *Red Badge of Courage* is attested to by many combat veterans as being a realistic portrayal of life and emotions at the front lines. The author can prepare himself through extensive reading, through contacts with those who have gone through the experience, through other types of research. Where the author's total lack of experience or knowledge is apparent, it should certainly be called to your reader's attention.

5. *Critical theories* — Some awareness of critical theories is important even in the impressionistic review; in the authoritative review it is a must. A review of a tragedy requires that the reviewer have some familiarity with the Aristotlean concept of the tragic hero, at the very least. The more extensive your knowledge of the various critical theories (e.g., the New Criticism), the greater force your review will have. It certainly would be worth your while

at least to become aware of the different theories. Ask your teacher or librarian for suggestions as to which books or articles to read.

FAMILIARITY WITH GENRE TO BE REVIEWED: Before you can hope to review any work, you must have a knowledge of the genre. For instance, to criticize Hemingway's "Old Man at the Bridge" because it lacks a plot would be an immediate revelation of your unawareness of the slice-of-life short story. You must know at least something about the art form you are reviewing. Be aware of the major characteristics of the novel, the short story, the play, the different types of poems, the essay, the biography. Be aware of the main differences and similarities between these genres. Be aware of some of the basic literary techniques that the author may employ. Know some of the literary and critical terminology of the various art forms to help you express your views effectively. *If you find that you have little or no knowledge of the genre you are to review, check with your teacher who will gladly suggest appropriate reading for you.*

THE AUDIENCE: There are two audiences with whom you must concern yourself: the audience to whom the work is directed and the audience for whom you are writing. In the first instance, unless the author has specified the audience whom he is trying to reach, it is for you to deduce the intended audience. In many instances this is rather self-evident. The level of language, the subject matter, the allusions within the work, the vocabulary, the formality or lack thereof, the manner in which the subject matter is treated, all reveal the intended audience. Sometimes the title by itself is sufficient; no one can doubt for whom *The Audiometric Assessment of Mentally Retarded Patients* by Dr. E. Harris Nober has been written; *The Bobbsey Twins and Their Schoolmates* is equally as revealing of its intended audience. The intended audience, then, and how successfully the author reaches that audience should be a matter of concern for you and something you will definitely want to discuss in your review.

The other audience, the audience for whom you are writing, is equally, if not more, important. Your whole approach to your review is in great part determined by your audience. The work cannot be judged in a vacuum; it must be judged by how it will appeal to your readers. If your readers are young elementary school children, you might readily suggest that they read the *Bobbsey Twins* book, but the chances of your recommending Dr. Nober's book to any but professionals are mighty slim. Certainly, what is good for one reader is not necessarily good for another.

There are other aspects of your audience that you should know not only before you review the work but also before you write the review:

1. *Age* — How old is the audience? Are they primarily high school students? college students?

2. *Intelligence* — What is the general level of intelligence? How widely read are they? What is their educational level?

3. *Background* — How diverse is their background? What similar experiences have they had? What are their attitudes? their prejudices? What are their likes and dislikes? Are they all part of the same nationality? ethnic group? religion? How familiar would they be with the subject matter of the work? How receptive would they be to the ideas expressed in the work?

These are some of the factors you must take into consideration before you write your review. Your approach to the work, your organization, your level of language, your choice of words, the depth of your analysis will all be affected by the audience with whom *you* want to communicate. This does not necessarily mean that you will change your views of the book, but it certainly means that you will consider your audience before determining whether or not to recommend the work. Your audience determines *how* you will say what you want to say.

READING OF OTHER REVIEWS: It will not hurt to consult other critics' views on the work under discussion. By all means, if time permits read as extensively as possible the critical opinions of others. But remember two essential points: (1) any opinions which did not originate with you must be properly credited and documented in your review, and (2) your review should be primarily the expression of *your* views. If you keep this in mind, you can then use the writings of others as an effective means to lend greater validity and force to your argument or you can use a contrasting and opposing viewpoint as an argumentative technique for presenting your views. However, *do not read other reviews until after you have read the work and formed your own opinion.*

PURPOSE OF THE REVIEW: At this point, before you begin the actual organization and writing of the review, it may be worthwhile to re-state its purpose. Its primary purpose is to express the reviewer's opinion concerning the work and, secondly, to tell your reader something about the work's content. In the first instance, your expression of opinion will probably focus on how successfully the author achieved his purpose in writing the work, an evaluation which you must effectively substantiate. Your evaluation may be geared to trying to persuade your reader to read — or to avoid reading — the work, or you may simply present your evaluation and let your reader come to his own decision. Either way, though, you should be determined to have some seriousness of attitude, to be fair to the author, and to have a positive effect on your reader. In the latter instance, you must remember that in all probability your reader has not read the work you are reviewing. *It, therefore, becomes necessary to give him some information about the work's content.* This does not mean though that the review consists of two separate parts: a summary of the contents and a paragraph or two of evaluation, or, worse yet, a long, detailed summary with a concluding statement that "This is a very good book and I think you should read it." This is neither criticism nor reviewing.

The summary of the book's content should be carefully interwoven with the critical observations. If you are concerned at all times with the substantiation of your opinion, you will of necessity have to refer to incidents from the work. These incidents, when selected with care, will give your reader a fairly good idea of what the work is all about. Don't hesitate to use quotations, to discuss the setting, to refer to effective scenes, to give details about a character, to give examples of humor, to give samples of the dialog *(see Chapter VII for specific suggestions for each genre)*. But always keep uppermost in your mind that *the primary function of the review is the expression of your opinion and that the details about the work are the means by which you substantiate that opinion.*

CHECKLIST: You may find the following checklist of value in preparing yourself to write your report:

1. Read the work to be reviewed with great care (see the reading Checklist on page 24).

2. Take careful notes as you read. Jot down these notes either in your own copy of the book or on slips of paper that you insert within the appropriate pages. Some items of concern might be:

    a. point of view

    b. title and preface

    c. organization

    d. style

    e. theme

    f. ending

    g. accuracy of information

    h. literary devices

    i. typography

3. To what extent are the following extrinsic factors (factors outside of the work) important in evaluating the work?

    a. biography — facets of the author's life

    b. literary period — the literary period or movement to which the work belongs

    c. author's intentions

    d. author's qualifications to deal with the subject matter

    e. critical theories — what do you need to know about the various critical theories in order to present a valid discussion and review of the work?

4. Be familiar with some of the basic characteristics of the genre you are reviewing.

5. Know something about the audience that, on the one hand, the author is aiming for, and, on the other hand, you are writing for. Before you write, consider your audience's

    a. age and sex

    b. intelligence and education

    c. background

6. Although not a necessity, read the views of other critics about the work, but only *after* you have read the work and formed your own opinion. Remember that any opinions which did not originate with you must be properly credited and documented.

7. Remember the twofold purpose of a review: (a) primarily to express your opinion of a work either in the hopes of persuading the reader to read — or not to read — the work or simply presenting your views and permitting your reader to make his own decision; (b) secondarily, since in

all probability your reader has not yet read the work, to give some information about the content of the work.

8. Interweave the information about the content of the work within your critical and evaluative remarks. The more effectively you can integrate the two, the better your review will be.

CHAPTER V

ORGANIZING THE REPORT

Once you have completed most of the preparations suggested in the preceding chapter, you should be ready to organize your review. Notice that it does not say *write* the review, but *organize,* for good writing is not accidental nor is it easy; it is a time-consuming, difficult undertaking but one which, when well done, can be highly rewarding. What greater thrill can there be than to communicate your ideas, thoughts, or feelings to others? Of course, this is only true if you are not writing simply to fulfill a course requirement; such themes often tend to be rather sterile. You must approach every writing experience as if you have just been commissioned to express your views in some well-known publication.

Organizing your paper — or any other piece of expository writing for that matter — involves four essential parts: (1) developing a thesis statement and preparing a careful outline which will develop that thesis, (2) writing a forceful introduction, (3) developing that introduction with a series of unified, coherent paragraphs which will prove the thesis, and, (4) concluding the essay in such an effective manner that the reader is certain that the argument has come to an end and that it is a logical outgrowth of the incidents presented in the body of the paper. Let us look at each of these parts separately.

THESIS AND OUTLINE: Before you begin formulating your thesis statement, carefully review all the marginal notes you have made, the notes you have jotted down on those slips of paper, and the passages you have underlined, and then think, think deeply about the work you have just read. Try to assimilate all the notes until you come up with a single impression, one hopefully which you feel deeply and which you will be able to communicate to your readers effectively. Once you have done that, you are ready to formulate your thesis statement.

The *thesis statement,* or the statement of theme as it is sometimes called, is the focal point of your outline for it concisely states your objective. You must write the thesis statement down after careful deliberation and revise and polish it until it finally encompasses your central idea, that single impression, to your satisfaction. Under no condition should you begin outlining before you are positive that the statement of thesis you have written down truly reflects your purpose in writing the report.

The thesis statement should be phrased as a statement and not as a question. Before finalizing it, however, keep in mind those factors which might affect the thesis, at least its scope: your audience, your awareness of extrinsic factors, length limitation, and writing time. In reviewing Hemingway's *The Sun Also Rises,* you might want to stress his style and its effect upon the work and theme; hence, your thesis statement might be: "Hemingway effectively portrays the futility and meaninglessness of life in *The Sun Also Rises* through his clipped style and structure and through his characters' dialog." Notice what limitations you have placed upon yourself. You must discuss in your report *how* the clipped style and structure and characters' dialog enable Hemingway to portray the futility and meaninglessness of life effectively. In your paper, you may not stray from that thesis. If after careful consideration that it is not to your liking, you might come up with this thesis: "Hemingway in *The Sun Also Rises* through careful character delineation paints a clear picture of the life styles of the expatriates in Paris following World War I." Or, your thesis might be: "Hemingway's *The Sun Also Rises* is a dull, boring account of the life styles of a group of 1920's hippies."

Notice carefully that each of these theses requires a different focus and different details from the book as substantiation. What your thesis will be is obviously up to you, but, at the risk of being repetitious, be certain before you begin outlining and writing that your stated thesis accurately reflects your aim; you may not change theses in the middle.

After you have formulated your thesis, you are ready to begin your *outline*. Since you have been thinking about the topic deeply, you should have a fairly good idea of the major arguments you will use to substantiate your thesis. However, at this point, you will first have to decide whether you will use an informal or a formal (Harvard) outline. The former lends itself best for short pieces of writing whereas the latter is extremely flexible in that it can be employed as readily for the outlining of a short theme as for a book.

The Harvard outline follows a rigid format: Roman numerals indicate major divisions (in the longer paper, they can indicate parts of the paper; in the shorter paper, paragraphs); upper case letters indicate sub-divisions; Arabic numerals further sub-divisions. For example:

    I.
   II.
  III.

        A.
        B.
        C.

            1.
            2.

                a.
                b.
                c.
                d.

                    (1)
                    (2)

> (a)
> (b)
> (c)

IV.

The indention must be exactly as above. *Furthermore, items should be expressed in parallel form:* If item I. is a prepositional phrase, then all Roman numeral items must be prepositional phrases; if A. is an infinitive, then all uppercase items must be infinitives. Also, there can never be just one sub-topic; there must be at least two or none, for sub-topics are sub-divisions, and no item can be divided into less than two parts.

Let us assume that your thesis is "Hemingway in *The Sun Also Rises* through careful character delineation paints a clear picture of the life styles of the expatriates in Paris following World War I." Since your focus here will be on characters in the book, you will probably list, as the first step in preparing your outline, the main characters: Jake Barnes, Lady Brett Ashley, Robert Cohn, Mike Campbell, Bill Gorton, and Pedro Romero. Your next step should be to find the details that will help you to substantiate your thesis.

At this point, you should write your notes on 4 x 6 index cards. You will find that cards are easier to handle, that it is easier to re-arrange the notes, and that once you begin writing the first draft it is easier to locate information than if you had taken notes on sheets of paper. Furthermore, you will find that this method of note-taking is a good habit to get into for it will force you to take notes in accordance with the outline headings and it will enable you to create sub-headings readily, listing these on separate cards.

For example, let us take the six main characters you have just listed. First, put the name of each at the top of a separate card. Now begin reviewing your notes in the book. Remember, that you are looking only for those details about the character portrayals which will give a picture of the expatriate's life in Paris. As you go over your textual jottings, you may find that the details seem to fall into distinct sub-divisions, e.g., *Lady Brett — physical characteristics; Robert Cohn — actions*. Make out a separate card for each of these sub-divisions and write down those notes which are relevant. This means that you are now becoming selective of what notes you copy from the book For each note you write down be certain to indicate the page number; you will need this later for documentation. If you quote, be certain that you are quoting accurately.

Once you have completed this process, see if perhaps the notes on the cards could be grouped in some other way than you originally envisioned. For example, you may decide that instead of discussing your thesis through each of the main characters, it might be more effective to deal with it through Hemingway's techniques of characterization: *dialog, character's actions, physical details, reactions to stimuli*. (If you so decide, you will now discover the benefits of having taken the notes on index cards.) Once you have made your decision, begin filling in the outline, always being fully aware that the order must be a logical development of the thesis.

After you have completed the outline, check each of the items against the thesis to see if the item is relevant and will help you to prove your thesis. If any item does not seem to be relevant or does not add something to proving the thesis, eliminate it. For example, you will find that you must eliminate all the notes on Pedro Romero for he cannot be classified as an expatriate. (By the way, do not forget to incorporate any relevant notes from sources outside of the book, always being careful to identify the source and the page numbers.) Now, review your outline once more to make certain that the remaining items are in logical order.

Once your outline has been completed, you are ready to begin writing the first draft of your report. But you must follow your outline scrupulously without any deviation whatsoever. Should you feel compelled while writing the paper to deviate, you can do so only if you revise the outline in its entirety. An outline which is not carefully followed serves no useful purpose whatsoever. It is akin to a building blueprint wherein the contractor makes changes as he goes along. The chances of either becoming a well-constructed work are negligible.

INTRODUCTION: The introductory paragraph is, perhaps, the most important part of the entire report and deservant of your greatest effort. It is this paragraph which will determine whether the reader will continue reading what you have to say. A dull, boring opening, such as "In this report I will discuss a book entitled *The Sun Also Rises* written by the author Ernest Hemingway," will prompt the reader to turn to another selection immediately. The introduction must be stimulating, vivid, alive, causing the reader to be anxious to read on. Always remember that you as a writer are in constant competition with all other writers, each vying for the reader's attention, a reader who is very selective. After all, you are probably the same type of reader. *In picking up a newspaper or magazine, you do not read all the selections; you choose.* And if you begin reading a selection which is dull or holds little promise, you stop reading and look for something else. Therefore, it will matter little how brilliant your argument becomes later on in the paper. If your introduction does not excite and stimulate your reader, you have lost him forever.

Besides being stimulating, the introduction must contain some basic information, not necessarily in the following order:

1. the essence of the thesis;

2. an implication of how you propose to develop that thesis, e.g., comparison/contrast, instances/examples;

3. the tone of the report (whimsical, satirical, formal, reflective, to name a few);

4. the title of the book and the author's name *(Caution:* Never begin with "This book..." even though the title of the book may be the title of your paper. The title of the paper is not technically an integral part of the paper; therefore, you may not use *this* since there is no antecedent to which *this* can refer.)

5. the major arguments you intend to employ in substantiating your thesis. On a purely mechanical level, each developmental sentence in the introductory paragraph could serve as a topic sentence for each paragraph within the theme.

As long as you keep in mind the importance of the introductory paragraph, there are several ways you may begin, the best one being the one that suits your thesis and tone most effectively. *Here are some possibilities:*

1. State your dominant idea immediately: "Dull, dull, dull! Hemingway's *The Sun Also Rises* is about as stimulating and exciting as a hot bath in the midst of a heat wave."

2. Place the work with reference to the author's previous writings, noting any change in subject matter, philosophy, tone.

3. Classify the work within the genre to which it belongs.

4. Relate some significant biographical information about the author which is significant to the work.

5. State the theme of the book or begin with a discussion of the author's purpose.

6. Discuss the author's qualifications — or lack thereof — for dealing with the subject.

7. Compare this work to others on the same subject written by different authors.

8. Give some significant historical background of the period during which the work is set.

9. Relate the work to a literary, social, or political movement.

10. Point out the significance of the work for us or some future generation.

11. Begin by quoting some passage from the book which is particularly interesting or significant.

12. Quote from the blurb, pointing out the inaccuracy and distortion.

13. Pinpoint the type of reader that the work will appeal to. Will it be a best seller or will it appeal only to a highly select audience?

14. Quote, cite, paraphrase, or refer to some other critical commentary of the work.

In the hands of the skillful writer, any one of these openings can be as effective as the next. However, if your writing experience is somewhat limited, you would do well to limit yourself beginning with the statement of your dominant idea. Such an opening will set the theme and tone right from the start for both you and your reader, and it will make you constantly aware, while you are writing, what your thesis is.

SAMPLE INTRODUCTIONS:

Dominant idea

>   For those interested in a clear, fascinating picture of the life styles of the expatriates in Paris during the 1920's, <u>The Sun Also Rises</u> is a must. Ernest Hemingway, through his deft characterizations of his main characters, makes us feel as if we too were experiencing the disillusionment and meaninglessness of life following World War I. The portrayals of Jake Barnes, of Lady Brett Ashley, of Robert Cohn, as well as those of Mike Campbell and Bill Gorton -- their actions and reactions, their mannerisms and their dialog, their hopes and their fears -- more than adequately demonstrate Hemingway's skill in making an era come alive for us.

Reference to other critical comments

    <u>Margaret Fleming</u>, a play dealing with the great moral problem of infidelity, was not too favorably received by the critics. Edward A. Dithmar, writing in the December 10, 1891 edition of the <u>New York Times</u>, rather succinctly expressed the consensus of his contemporaries by stating that James A. Herne's play was the ". . . quintessence of the commonplace. Its language is the colloquial English of the shops and the streets and the kitchen fire-place. Its personages are the every-day non-entities that some folks like to forget when they go to the theatre. . . . The life it portrays is sordid and mean, and its effect upon a sensitive mind is depressing. . . . The stage would be a stupid and useless thing if such plays as <u>Margaret Fleming</u> were to prevail . . . /for/ love is a mean thing in his play." But how wrong Dithmar and his fellow critics were! Herne's play is a distinguished example of a sociological drama, and its simplicity and sincerity, as well as its characters -- characters who are not types

but individuals, real people -- make <u>Margaret</u>
<u>Fleming</u> one of the outstanding plays of that era.
It was a far cry from the earlier melodrama.
Realism in the theater had finally become a reality.

Classification within the genre

With the presentation of the Pulitzer Prize
winning play <u>Beyond the Horizon</u> in 1920, it be-
came apparent that a new force had arrived in
the American theater; one, who, through the medi-
um of the play, had made a real contribution to
the knowledge of life, and who established playwriting in America among the fine arts by bringing to playwriting an artistic integrity and a
disciplined craftsmanship. It was in this play
that Eugene O'Neill challenged the attention of
those who could recognize an original and power-
ful note in the drama.

Statement of author's purpose

Primarily, Van Wyck Brooks is concerned
with tracing the literary and intellectual development and history between the years 1865
and 1915. The subject of <u>New England: Indian
Summer</u>, as he states it, is "The New England
mind as it has found expression in the lives
and works of writers." He further states that
he has been brief in his treatment of recent
and living authors (except in two or three cases),
his chief concern being the background from which
they emerged. It is obvious that Mr. Brooks not
only succeeded in fulfilling his objective, but
also succeeded admirably. He demonstrates a
comprehensive knowledge of his subject, and com-
municates this knowledge interestingly and de-
lightfully.

Reference to previous writings

The Town is the second book of a trilogy
in which William Faulkner traces the rise of the
Snopeses, Flem Snopes in particular, a repellent
specimen of white trash who has his first triumphs in The Hamlet when he marries the pregnant
daughter of Will Varner, the somewhat feudal lord
of Frenchman's Bend. In The Town, Flem continues
his upward climb in Jefferson through his shrewd
business sense but mainly as the result of Mayor
de Spain's sexual attachment for Mrs. Snopes. The
story, effectively though at times confusingly
told through the narrations of Gavin Stevens,
Charles Mallison, and V.K. Ratliff, concerns itself with the strongly opposing values of Flem
Snopes and Gavin Stevens, the changing values
against the entire time-honored traditions of the
South.

DEVELOPMENT — THE BODY: Once you have whetted your reader's appetite with your introductory paragraph, you must now strive to retain his interest with every single paragraph that follows. Always keep uppermost in your mind that the reader is fickle, that he can stop reading anytime he becomes bored, and there is absolutely no way that you can bring him back. The function of the introduction was to get the reader's attention; the function of each succeeding paragraph is to keep the reader there, eager to hear what you have to say next.

The outline and the method of development will determine the body of the paper. *The paper of comparison and/or contrast,* for example, will develop its thesis by comparing and/or contrasting two factors (e.g., the work under discussion with another work by the same author, two techniques of character development, two different methods of developing the same theme). *The paper of definition* on the other hand, will most likely be used in defining the genre within which the work falls. Regardless though of the basic method of development — be it *comparison/contrast, instances/examples, cause and effect, definition, anecdotes, steps in a process,* or a *combination* of these — it is unlikely that every paragraph will be developed in the same manner. Taking that paper of comparison and contrast, for example, you will most likely develop some paragraphs by instances and examples, some by cause and effect, some by anecdote, and some by comparison.

On a purely mechanical level, each paragraph in your theme could be the development of a sentence in the introductory paragraph:

> *Introductory paragraph:* Topic sentence
> Sentence 1
> Sentence 2
> Sentence 3
> Sentence 4
> Concluding sentence

Development:

Paragraph 1: Topic sentence = sentence 1
               Sentence A
               Sentence B
               Sentence C
               Concluding sentence

Paragraph 2: Topic sentence = sentence 2
               Sentence D
               Sentence E
               Sentence F
               Sentence G
               Concluding sentence

Paragraph 3: Topic sentence = sentence 3

Paragraph 4: Topic sentence = sentence 4

Concluding paragraph

Keep in mind however, that such a purely mechanical method of development could create a very dull and stilted paper.

Of prime importance in the development of your thesis is adequate substantiation. Do not be afraid to rely heavily on quotations, paraphrases, incidents, and anecdotes from the work. Integrate these effectively into your critical commentaries so that you do not have a portion of the paper dealing with the book's contents and a separate portion dealing with your critical observations. An effectively developed report is one in which critical observations are effectively substantiated and in which the substantiation is woven into the critical commentary.

CONCLUSION: The importance of the concluding paragraph is surpassed only by that of the introduction. Do not let your report merely stop as if you had nothing more to say or as if you forgot to write the ending. The concluding paragraph lets your reader know in no uncertain terms that the argument has been presented in its entirety and that you are satisfied that you have proved your thesis. The well-organized argument comes to its conclusion logically and naturally. If you find yourself having to say "in conclusion" or "to sum up," or any other comparable phrase, you are, in fact, suggesting that the ending is weak and that your reader needs to be told that he is reading the conclusion. Although a re-phrasing of the introduction — re-stating the dominant impression, summarizing your main arguments, stating your final judgment of the work — is better than no ending at all, the test of the good ending is simple: *if it were at the bottom of the page, would the reader be tempted to turn to the next page for the continuation?* If no, the ending was strong, forceful, and final. Remember that the ending is the last thought you leave with the reader, so end on a strong note.

One final word of caution: the concluding paragraph is not the place to introduce a new idea or to contradict your thesis.

CHECKLIST: Use the following checklist in organizing your report:

1. Carefully review all your notes in the work — marginal, slips of paper, underlined portions. Think deeply about the work *until you come up with a single impression.*

2. Formulate your statement of thesis. Write it down, revising it until the statement is an accurate reflection of your main idea.

3. Begin your outline by listing its major divisions.

4. Using 4 x 6 index cards, check through the textual notes once again, listing those notes which will substantiate your thesis. Eliminate all others. Use separate cards for each division and sub-division.

5. Basing it on your notes, complete the outline.

6. Check each item in the outline against the thesis statement, making certain that each item is relevant and will help you to substantiate the thesis.

7. In writing your paper, follow the outline scrupulously. Make no changes.

8. Pay special attention to the introduction to your paper. It should encompass the following:

    a. the essence of the thesis,

    b. an implication of how you propose to develop the thesis,

    c. the tone of the paper,

    d. the title of the work and the author's name,

    e. the major arguments you intend to employ in substantiating the thesis.

9. Be aware of the different ways in which you can begin (see pages 44-50).

10. Develop the introduction through a series of related paragraphs, with *special emphasis on substantiating your thesis*. Use quotations; paraphrase; cite!

11. Interweave your statements about the book's content within your critical observations. Do *not* have two separate parts: something about the book's content and some critical observations.

12. Write a conclusion which is forceful and dynamic, one which lets your reader know in no uncertain terms that you have brought your argument to a logical end.

13. Do *not* use "in conclusion," "to sum up" or any other comparable phrase in your concluding paragraph. And never, never write "the end" or "finis" at the end of the paper.

CHAPTER VI

WRITING THE REPORT

You have completed reading the work; you have thought about it; you have taken notes; you have organized your thoughts; you have formulated your thesis statement; and you have carefully outlined your report. Now comes the time to sit down and write since all the ground work has been completed. This is the true test where you must now communicate your thoughts and feelings to your readers logically and coherently. Of course, the more deeply you feel about the work, the easier you will find it to express yourself. But one way or the other, the following suggestions should make the writing of the report easier for you and, hopefully, reduce the pile of crumpled sheets of paper in your wastebasket.

WRITING THE FIRST DRAFT: Your first draft is your *working draft,* one which you will *correct, revise,* and *modify.* If you have no intention of making revisions, you might as well make your first draft your final copy. However, the chances of your writing an effective paper are extremely slim. It is the rough draft which gives you your first opportunity to flesh out the skeleton of your review.

Before you begin writing, check your outline over one more time. Carefully re-read your thesis statement, making certain that it is an accurate statement of your dominant impression. Then check each item in the outline against the thesis to make certain that the item is relevant and adds something to the further development of your argument. Make certain that there are ample references from the book to substantiate your thesis adequately. Check the order of the items to make certain that you are developing your argument logically. Any changes that you want to make in the outline must be made now. Once you are satisfied that each of the above conditions has been met, you are ready to begin writing.

Most students will prefer to write their first draft in longhand. If you are one of these, supply yourself with a sheaf of wide-lined paper — the legal-size paper is recommended — and pen. *Write on alternate lines or, even better, on every third line, thus giving yourself ample room for revisions.* In addition, leave ample margins on both left and right. In other words, write in such a way that you will not hesitate to make changes later on. Write clearly and legibly, paying attention to correct sentence structure, paragraphing, spelling, and all other rules of grammar and mechanics, but not to the point where it will interfere with your concentration on the content. Number your pages consecutively in the upper right hand corner.

If you are among the few who find it easier to type the first draft, supply yourself with unlined paper — any color will do. Triple space your copy and leave wide margins on all four sides. Here, as in the longhand written copy, write on one side of the paper only and number the pages consecutively. Since this will be a rough draft, don't hesitate to x-out portions you want to disregard.

Regardless of whether you write or type your first draft, have the following books on your desk for easy referral:

1. A good desk dictionary (one which has been revised within the past five years) so that you can check your spelling, proper word usage, and syllabification.

2. Roget's *Thesaurus* to help you find the "right" word or to prevent you from using the same one over and over again.

3. A good writer's handbook on grammar and usage so that you can check grammatical structures, punctuation, and any other aspect of correct writing and structure. Your class grammar text will probably serve this purpose.

Do not hesitate to refer to these sources as often as the need arises. The greater the attention you pay to the mechanical and grammatical aspects now, the more effort you can devote to the important element of style in your revision.

As you write your rough draft, remember the suggestions in the preceding chapter, particularly those dealing with the introduction, body, and conclusion of the report. Also remember that the first draft should be complete, though necessarily unpolished. This means that you must write out any quotations fully and where necessary write out the footnotes as well for it is possible that you may have to make corrections here too.

SOME ASPECTS OF STYLE: This section makes no attempt to present a complete discussion of all aspects of style nor does it pretend to be a grammar and usage text. For a reference source that will deal with all aspects of style, grammar, and correct usage, refer, as frequently as necessary, to a good grammar text. All that is intended here is to make you cognizant of some of the more troublesome areas.

Coherence and unity—In order for a piece of writing to be readily understood by a reader, it must be unified and coherent. That is to say, every item, every thought must be relevant to the thesis and all these items must be logically related to each other.

The unity of a paper is maintained by carefully organizing one's thoughts into paragraphs — each paragraph expressing a separate idea through a series of related sentences developing the idea which was expressed or implied in the topic sentence. You must be sure that each paragraph — and each sentence within the paragraph — is relevant to your thesis. If you find that any idea does not aid in the development of the thesis, then that idea —regardless of how interesting it may be in its own right— does not belong in a unified paper.

Unity in a paper does not necessarily imply coherence. Coherence can be achieved by several techniques: use of transitional words or phrases (e.g., *on the other hand, in addition, neverthless, furthermore); repetition of key words or phrases; partial restatement of ideas; use of synonyms for key words; use of parallel grammatical structure; consistent use of the same point of view, and logical organization. It is the coherence which will enable the reader to follow your argument easily and logically.

After you have asked yourself whether each thought and idea is relevant to the thesis statement and whether it *adds* something to that which has already been said, you should ask yourself one additional question: *Does it logically follow that which precedes it and is it properly joined to the thought or idea that follows?* If the answer is yes, then your paper will be coherent.

Point of view—Point of view is the term generally used to indicate the point from which the paper is written, that is, first person, third person, or omniscient. In very formal papers, the first person, singular, "I," is avoided by some writers who refer to themselves in the third person, singular, e.g., "the author," "the writer." Usage today, however, favors the less formal and stiff "I," which you should use especially in an impressionistic review.

Sentence structure—

1. *Errors in structure:* Two of the most common errors in sentence structure, the run-on or comma-splice and the fragment, must be avoided at all costs. To be sure, either one of these may be used stylistically, but you must exercise the greatest caution. When used correctly, the run-

on and the fragment are very effective, but if used incorrectly, they are serious errors.

The run-on is primarily an error in punctuation; that is to say, two thoughts are run together without proper punctuation separating them. The run-on sentence can be corrected in three ways: (1) by placing a period at the end of the first thought and capitalizing the first word of the second thought; (2) by placing a semi-colon between the two thoughts; and (3) by using a comma *and* a coordinating conjunction *(and, but, for, nor, or, get, so)* between the two thoughts.

The fragment is an incompletely stated thought whose incompleteness may be due to the omission of the subject, the verb, or the complement. It may also be due to using a verbal in place of a verb or by not completing a thought begun with a dependent clause. Correct the fragment by supplying the missing part.

Other errors in structure include the dangling or misplaced modifier, awkward phrasing, and lack of parallel structure. If you suspect that your sentence contains any one of these, refer to your handbook for proper methods of correction.

2. *Subordination:* Subordination is the technique of placing the less important thought in a subordinate position. The dominant idea should always be expressed in the main clause. Subordinate clauses can be adverbial, adjectival, or substantive (noun) in function. In other words, these groups of words, containing a subject and verb, can function in the sentence in the same manner as an adverb, adjective, or noun. Subordinate thoughts which are not important enough to contain subject and verb should be expressed in phrases.

3. *Variety:* It is variety in sentence structure and sentence opening which avoids monotony, makes the paper more readable, and enables the writer to express himself

more effectively through the nuances in meaning reflected by the structure.

Basic structure of the sentence can be varied by compounding ideas or subordinating one idea to another. It can further be effected by using items in series, by using a series of short sentences, by effective use of involved, involuted sentence structure; by rearranging the normal subject-verb-complement pattern, and by varying sentence length.

Variations of sentence openings can be achieved by beginning a sentence with an adverbial clause, a prepositional phrase, a verbal (participle, gerund, infinitive) phrase, an expletive (a word such as *there* which has no grammatical function in the sentence), a parenthetical expression *(in fact, on the other hand),* an adverb, an adjective, or a coordinate conjunction. Be cautioned that although any of the above will give you variety, they cannot be used interchangeably, for each variation will affect the meaning of the sentence.

4. *Abbreviations:* Do *not* use any in the writing of reports.

5. *Numbers:* Generally, all numbers which consist of one or two words are written out. In addition, *any* number which is the first word in a sentence must be written out.

Numerals are used for (1) numbers consisting of more than two words, (2) sums of money, (3) numbers in addresses and dates, (4) numbers used to express time of day when used with a.m. and p.m. but not with *o'clock* and (5) page numbers, volume numbers, and chapter and verse numbers.

6. *Italics:* Italics in typed and handwritten manuscripts are indicated by underlining the item to be italicized with an unbroken line.

(a) *Emphasis:* Italics may be used (in lieu of quotation marks or capitalization) to stress a word or phrase in the text. However, use it sparingly to maintain its effectiveness. If you wish to stress a word or phrase within a direct quotation, you may also use italics. But you must then state in brackets — not parentheses — that you have supplied the italics, e.g., [italics mine].

(b) *Foreign terms:* Foreign terms which have not been anglicized must be italicized. Since there is disagreement, in some cases, as to which terms have been anglicized, use a recent edition of a dictionary as your guide.

(c) *Titles:* Titles of full-length books, newspapers, magazines, periodicals, unpublished manuscripts are italicized. Titles of works which are part of a collection (e.g., short story titles) are placed within quotation marks.

(d) *Italicized words in sources:* Words or phrases which appear in italics in the source to be quoted must be underlined when quoted.

6. *Contractions:* Contractions in formal writing are generally avoided. In the informal essay, it is permissible for you to contract verb and adverb *(haven't)*, but do not contract subject and verb *(I've, we're)*.

7. *Syllabification:* Whenever possible, words should not be hyphenated, that is, split between two lines. Where it becomes necessary, be certain that the break occurs at the end of a syllable.

8. *Punctuation:* Refer to your handbook for all rules for the proper use of punctuation marks. Here, however, are some rules which need special emphasis:

(a) *Final punctuation:* Only one final punctuation mark is used. At no time should you use a double period, or a question mark followed by a period. The only exception would occur where the sentence ends with an abbreviation; then the period indicating the abbreviated form is followed by the question mark or the exclamation point, but never by another period.

(b) *Punctuation preceding final quotation mark:*
The comma and period *always precede* the final quotation
mark. All other punctuation marks precede the final quotation mark when they are part of the quotation, and
follow the mark when they are not.

(c) *Parentheses and brackets in quotations:* Brackets and parentheses are not to be confused. Brackets are
to be used only for the insertion of editorial comment
within a quotation. Anything appearing within parentheses is part of the original quotation.

(d) *Ellipsis:* The omission of any part of a quotation is indicated by three spaced dots (...). When the
omission occurs at the end of a sentence, a fourth dot re-
presenting the period is added.

9. *Tense:* For a detailed discussion of the function,
form, and correct use of tense, mood, and voice, you must
again avail yourself of your handbook. However, the following points are worthy of stress:

(a) *Past tense:* Generally speaking, most papers
are written in the past tense, although the historical present may be used for emphasis and a sense of immediacy.
Use this form sparingly.

(b) *Present tense:* Aside from its use in the historical present, the present tense is also employed in critical comments — but not in biographical references where
the subject is deceased — and in stating universal truths.
There is a distinct difference, for example, between saying
"*Hamlet* was one of the greatest plays" and "*Hamlet* is
one of the greatest plays." Note, therefore, that your judgments concerning the work you are discussing should be
in the present tense.

(c) *Past perfect tense:* The past perfect tense (e.g.,
had worked) is used to indicate an action completed before another action completed. In the statement, "Oedipus
had killed his father and married Jocasta," the past perfect *had killed* indicates that the killing of the father pre-
ceded the marrying of Jocasta.

(d) *Consistency:* Although changes in tense are permissible, you must be careful not to shift tense haphazardly. Unnecessary shifts in tense, aside from affecting clarity and style, will ruin the unity of the paper.

10. *Reference of pronouns:* Exercise great care when you use a pronoun that you have either stated or clearly implied a definite antecedent. Pronouns must agree with their antecedents in person, gender, and number. When using such indefinite pronouns as *anyone, everyone, someone, anybody,* you must use the third person, singular, masculine gender (functioning as common gender — both male and female). Unnecessary shifts in person should be avoided.

11. *Paragraphing:* Since clarity of meaning is, to a great extent, dependent upon the logical expression of units of thought, you must organize your paragraphs effectively. Be aware of basic paragraph organization — topic sentence, developmental sentences, concluding sentence — and of the various methods of paragraph development. Also pay close attention to paragraph unity and coherence and to proper transition from one paragraph to the next.

12. *Vocabulary:* Words convey meaning and the broader a writer's vocabulary base, the easier it will be for him to express his thoughts accurately. Be cautioned against slavish dependence on the *Thesaurus,* searching out so-called "big" words because you feel they will be impressive. Choose your words carefully and use that word which best suits the idea.

13. *Spelling:* The only suggestion that can be offered here is that when in doubt, check your dictionary for the correct, preferred spelling, even if it means checking every word.

14. *Wordiness:* Writers of papers, especially student writers, have a tendency to be extremely verbose in the presentation of their ideas. Perhaps this wordiness has been fostered over the years by teachers who have assigned

papers of varying lengths or who seemed to judge quality by quantity. But number of words alone does not reflect understanding or insight. Be concise! If you find that a paragraph can be condensed to a sentence, do so. If the sentence can be condensed to a subordinate clause, the clause to a phrase, the phrase to a word, and if the word can be eliminated altogether, do so. Then if you have a thousand word paper, it will be a thousand meaningful words.

REVISING THE FIRST DRAFT: After you have finished writing the first draft, set it aside for several days so that when you return to it you can approach it with a degree of objectivity. *If you re-read your paper immediately you will discover that you are not actually reading what you have written, but what you think you have written.* Also read your paper out loud at least once and listen to what you have said. Does it *sound* logical? Does it read well?

This is the time to make use of those wide margins and skipped lines. Do not check and correct only the mechanical errors, but also check for structure and style. Do not hesitate to re-write sentences and even paragraphs, if it is warranted. Check for accuracy of quotations, for proper documentation, and for inadvertent plagiarism. Make certain that you have presented your argument forcefully and coherently. Check for paragraph and theme unity. Make sure that you have presented adequate substantiation of your thesis. Be certain that you have avoided wordiness, repetition, and irrelevant matter. Check your ending: is it forceful? is it based on the arguments presented throughout the paper? And last but not least, are you pleased with the paper? Would you be proud to have this review read anywhere by anyone?

If you find that your draft looks rather messy at this point, take it as a sign that you have actively revised. Do not hesitate to make a second draft that is legible and can be copyread once more before you write your final copy. Do not begin writing your final copy until such time that you are certain that this review is one of the best pieces of writing you have done. Once you are convinced of that, re-read the draft once more for any errors you might have missed. Now you are ready to write your final copy.

THE FINAL MANUSCRIPT: Unless your teacher gives you specific directions for preparation of the final manuscript, follow these suggestions.

1. *Typed manuscripts:* It is always preferable to type any paper, but only if you know how to type. Typed manuscripts that are filled with erasures and x-ed out portions are to be avoided at all costs. *Should you have someone type the paper for you, remember that the finished product is your responsibility; any errors are yours.*

If you are planning to type your paper, adhere to the following:

a. *Paper:* Use a good grade of white 8½ x 11 bond. Erasable bond is recommended for it will enable you to make erasures without leaving smudges. (Your may, instead of making erasures, use correcting tape.) Do *not* use lined paper.

b. *Typewriter:* Make certain that the typewriter is in good working order and that the keys have been cleaned recently. The ribbon must be either blue or black (no red, please) and should still have sufficient ink for a uniformly clear imprint. Avoid changing ribbons in the midst of the report.

c. *Margins:* Margins on all four sides of the sheet of paper should be equal. If you plan to staple or bind your report along the left-hand margin, make that margin wider. Be sure that top and bottom margins on all sheets are constant. You will, of course, encounter greater difficulty in maintaining the right-hand margin; however, careful planning will minimize its irregularity.

d. *Spacing:* All typed manuscripts, with the exception of footnotes, bibliographical entries, quotations set off from the text, and book review headings, are double spaced. *Type on one side of the paper only.*

e. *General:* A typed manuscript must be typed throughout. You should not make any insertions in pen and ink.

2. *Handwritten manuscripts:* If typing your paper is not possible, you must write it in longhand. If your handwriting tends to be illegible, plan to take extra time to form your letters as neatly as possible. Be certain to distinguish between upper and lower case letters; cross your *t*'s and dot your *i*'s; and do not make your letters so small that one needs a magnifying glass to read your writing. There is little sense in devoting all the time you did in the preparation of your report if your final copy proves to be illegible.

a. *Paper:* If you have mastered the art of writing in horizontal parallel lines, you may use white *unlined* 8½ x 11 paper; if not, use white lined paper with a ruled left-hand margin. Avoid the narrow-spaced paper and, if possible, use paper without loose-leaf perforations.

b. *Margins:* The wide top margin and the ruled left margin are sufficient. Right-hand margin should be one inch (do not draw in the margin) and the bottom margin should be the last one and one-half spaces.

c. *Spacing:* Write on every line, beginning on the second line (the first space) at the top of the page. Skip one line between paragraphs. Write on one side of the paper only.

d. *Pen and ink:* You may use either ball point or pen and ink, but be certain that your pen won't run out during the writing of the paper. If it does, use a pen with the same type of point and the same color ink. If possible, avoid the felt tipped pens. Use blue or black ink only.

3. *General directions for both typed and handwritten manuscripts:* The following directions are applicable regardless of whether you type the manuscripts or not:

    a. *Heading:* Unless otherwise directed, use the book review heading which incorporates the following:

      (1) Title of the book, underlined and followed by a period.

      (2) The author's full name. Do not include any titles, e.g., professor, doctor. Follow his name with a period.

      (3) The place of publication, followed by a colon.

      (4) Publisher's name, followed by a comma.

      (5) Year of publication, followed by a period.

      (6) Number of pages, followed by a period.

All this information is written along the top margin, from left to right and single spaced. Now double space (or skip a line) and centered on the next line, write your by-line.

Sample heading — typed manuscript:

The Hamlet. By William Faulkner. New York: Random

House, 1931. 373 pages.

      By Frank Maziah

Sample heading — handwritten manuscript:

	The Hamlet. By William
	Faulkner. New York :
	Random House, 1931. 373 pages.
	By Frank Maziah

b. *Pagination:* There is no need to number the first page. If your prefer to do so, place the number at the bottom of the page, centered on the line and enclosed in dashes, e.g., —1—. On succeeding pages, number either at the center of the top margin and enclosed in dashes, or at the right-hand corner of the top margin, followed by a period. Choose one method and follow it consistently. There should be no heading on succeeding pages.

c. *Footnoting:* If you are quoting from the work being reviewed, all you need do is place the page number in parentheses following the quotation, e.g., "He made it in nineteen minutes, hurtling and bouncing among the ruts ahead of his spinning dust..." (358). If the quotation is from some other source, or if you use someone else's ideas, document your source with correct footnotes. Although footnotes should technically appear at the bottom of the page, in short works such as a review it is permissible to add a separate sheet entitled *Footnotes* at the end of the paper.

For correct footnote entries, see:

Teitelbaum, Harry. *How To Write Theses*. New York: Monarch Press, 1975. Chapter VIII.

Or check with your teacher for other manuals to use.

d. *Making a copy:* It is highly recommended that you always keep a copy, preferably a carbon copy of any manuscript that you submit. Keep this copy until such time as the original is returned to you.

e. *Final reading:* Before you collate your paper, read the final copy over very carefully for typographical errors. Do not hesitate to re-write or re-type the page if you must make more than a couple of minor corrections.

f. *Collating:* Place the sheets in consecutive order and, unless otherwise directed, staple in either the upper left-hand corner or along the left-hand margin (two or three staples will be more than adequate). If you prefer, insert the finished manuscript in a thesis folder. However, do *not* paste these pages on construction paper or in any other way *decorate* your report.

CHECKLIST: Use this checklist when writing your report:

1. Write your first draft on every third line and leave wide margins for later revisions. Concentrate on content and on following the outline carefully.

2. Keep basic reference tools handy and use them.

3. Before revising the first draft, let at least one day lapse so that you can approach your paper objectively. Read it out loud at least once. Make all necessary corrections, re-writing entire portions if necessary.

4. If you made many corrections, do not hesitate to write a second draft. Carefully copyread this.

5. Once *all* corrections and revisions have been made, and you are convinced that this is your best writing, you are ready to write your final copy.

6. Decide whether you will type or write the final copy in longhand. Follow the directions and suggestions outlined on pages 65-69.

7. Keep a copy of your paper.

8. Copyread once more before collating your paper. If necessary, re-write or re-type any page that has more than a couple of minor corrections.

9. Collate your paper.

CHAPTER VII

REVIEWING THE DIFFERENT GENRES

Although all literary reviews require the same focus on the reviewer's opinion of the work substantiated with ample evidence from the work, you will find that each genre, be it novel, play, biography, or any other literary form, will necessitate a slightly different approach and emphasis. Among other factors, as has been discussed here earlier, you must have a fairly good understanding of the characteristics of the genre to which the work being reviewed belongs. You should know what skills are demanded of the author and what effect variations in the genre's characteristics will have. In this way you will be able to judge more validly if the *how* of what the author says reinforces the *what* and if it does so effectively.

As a student you will, at one time or another, be called upon to write reports on the following major literary classifications: *novels, biographies, plays, non-fiction prose* (other than biographies), and *collections of shorter works.* Let us look more closely at what a review of each of these would entail.

THE NOVEL: The term *novel* is an all-inclusive word that describes any long (?) work of fiction written, generally, in prose. Under this umbrella term you will find such variations as classical, Romantic, impressionistic, realistic, Gothic, and naturalistic novels as well as historical novels, fantastic novels, adventure novels, and psychological novels, to name but a few. Here again each will require some slightly different approach in reviewing. For

71

example, to pan Swift's *Gulliver's Travels* for its gross exaggerations would be ludicrous and an admission that the reviewer has no awareness of the essential characteristic of the fantastic novel — fantasy as a means of emphasis. Yet the characteristics of the novel are sufficiently similar that we can use some common guidelines for writing reviews.

Below are aspects of the work that you can discuss under the two elements of the review: critical observations (your impression of the work's worth) and some facts about the book's content. But remember that in the review these two parts must be integrated, with the latter subordinate to the former.

Critical observations:

1. The style — forcefulness, clarity, use of symbolism, allegory, satire, appropriateness to subject and theme.

2. Author's theme or purpose — How apparent is it? Is the novel primarily a vehicle for propaganda? How effectively is the theme developed? Is the primary purpose of the novel to entertain?

3. Author's diction — How effective is his choice of words? Do they set the tone and mood? What is the level of language? Is it appropriate to the story? Is it primarily used for shock value?

4. Degree of difficulty — Does the subject matter or the diction in any way limit the audience appeal? Is it too difficult or too simple? If it is very difficult, is it worthwhile "struggling" through the novel?

5. Audience — For what type of audience was the novel seemingly written? What is the work's appeal? Will it be a best seller? Is its appeal limited to a highly intellectual group? Might the work become a classic? To what tastes does the work appeal?

6. Mood and tone — Whimsical? Satirical? Mock heroic? Reflective? Tragic? Comic?

7. Development — Is the story adequately developed? Overdeveloped? Too superficial?

8. Author's knowledge — How qualified is the author to write about the subject? What experiences has he had? How much of the success of the novel is dependent on the reader's awareness of the autobiographical nature of the work?

9. Comparison and/or contrast with other books by the same author — How does this novel rate in comparison to other writings by the author?

10. Comparison and/or contrast with other books of the same genre or topic by different authors.

11. Comparison and/or contrast of the same work to a different genre — How does the movie version compare to the book? The novel to the diary on which it was based?

Facts about the book's content:

1. The plot — What is the situation? the complication? How is the plot developed? What is the climax? Is the ending effective?

2. Interesting incidents — Discuss one or two interesting incidents used in the plot development.

3. Humorous or dramatic scenes — Briefly discuss one or two, showing why they are humorous or dramatic.

4. Setting — Give examples of the setting and show its effectiveness or lack thereof. What use does the author make of time and place? How "real" is the setting?

5. Character delineation — Are the characters developed in depth? Do they seem real? Are they superficial? Are they psychological disembodiments? How are the characters developed? Do our attitudes towards the characters change?

6. Show the contrasts or similarities between two characters.

7. Is the protagonist a tragic hero? Is he an anti-hero?

8. What is the author's attitude towards his protagonist?

9. How does the author present women? Members of minority groups?

10. What is the author's attitude towards life? interpersonal human relationships? government? religion?

The above are some of the aspects that you can deal with in reviewing the novel; however, you must be fully aware that you have to be highly selective in which of these you will choose. The information you give about the book's content will be determined to a great extent by your critical observations. Needless to say, you cannot, nor should you attempt to, discuss all of these aspects.

A careful reading of the two listings will also make you aware that the two categories tend to overlap, that it is difficult to separate the something about the book's content from the critical observations. And that's how it should be.

One last word of caution in reviewing a novel: Do not write a summary of the book. Choose carefully those incidents which will help you to substantiate your dominant impression. The only time you might want to reveal the book's ending is if you want to be certain that your reader will not read the novel. If that is the case, then by all means tell him that it was the butler who did it. But keep in mind that among professional reviewers, there is a feeling that the plot — especially its resolution — is the author's sacred property, to be revealed only to the reader who has *earned* it by reading the original in its entirety.

THE PLAY: Much of what has been said in the discussion of the novel is equally applicable to the play with one major difference: The play is meant to be seen rather than read. As such, much of a play's appeal may be visual with the characters' actions and movements and with such stage mechanics as setting, costuming, light and sound effects adding to or detracting from its overall success. For example, the mood is often created by the stage setting (as it is in Miller's *Death of a Salesman*), or much of the humor in a play is determined by the character's actions accompanying the dialog rather than by the dialog itself. However, since you will most likely be called upon to write reports on plays that you have read rather than seen, you will limit yourself to discussing the effectiveness of the written form, although you can introduce how staging might affect the work's success.

In reviewing the play, you will again concern yourself with the two elements of critical observations and some facts about the play's content. (Since many of these guidelines are the same as those for the novel, refer to pages 72-74 for the details when none are given below.)

Critial observations:

1. The style — Is the play written in prose or verse? If in verse, how effective is it?

2. Author's theme or purpose

3. Author's diction — In the play, dialog of the characters is of prime importance. Can you recognize the different characters by what they say and how they say it? Is the dialog stilted? Are there too many long speeches? Is the dialog too choppy? Does it sound "real"?

4. Degree of difficulty — Must the play be seen in order to be understood?

5. Audience

6. Mood and tone

7. Development — Is there unity of time? unity of action? If the author has "violated the unities," has he done so with artistic intent and success?

8. Author's knowledge

9. Comparison and/or contrast with other works by the same author — Is this his first play?

10. Comparison and/or contrast with other plays by different authors.

11. Comparison and/or contrast of the play to a different genre — Is the novel form of this work more effective? Did the play lend itself more to a screen version?

12. Action — Is the action apparent from the dialog? Are stage directions adequate? Are the characters static on the stage?

13. Type of play — tragedy, comedy, farce, melodrama, fantasy, burlesque. What critical theories, if any does the playwright follow? Is the type appropriate to the subject matter?

Facts about the play's content:

1. The plot

2. Interesting scenes or incidents within scenes

3. Humorous or dramatic scenes

4. Setting — Besides time and place, analyze the proposed stage setting as revealed either through the dialog or through stage directions.

5. Character delineation

6. Show the contrast or similarities between two characters. Analyze the protagonist's character foil, if there is one.

7. Is the protagonist a tragic hero? an anti-hero?

8. What is the author's attitude towards his protagonist?

9. How does the author portray his various characters? What are his prejudices?

10. What is the author's attitude towards life? interpersonal human relationships? government? religion?

Remember that reading a play requires special skills, skills that you should master before you review the work. *Always be aware of your own limitations as a reader so that you take these into account before passing judgment.*

BIOGRAPHIES: The primary function of the biography is to present the subject's life, or some facet of it, in an interesting manner so that the reader may learn from it, and hopefully become enlightened by it. One function, then, of the biography moreso than that of any other genre (with the exception of the non-fiction prose) is to teach. Your emphasis in the review might very well be on how effectively the biographer accomplishes that function.

Ideally, as a reviewer you should have some familiarity with the subject of the biography. In that way you will be able to judge the accuracy of detail, the biographer's insights and judgments, and what new light the biographer may shed on the subject's life. If you lack this knowledge, you must then concentrate on how the work is written and on how it appeals to others with backgrounds similar to yours. *Of great importance, however, is for you to remember that you are reviewing the book and not the life of the subject.* Concentrate your critical remarks on the biography. The biography can be excellent even though the subject may be despicable.

Critical observations:

1. The style — (See suggestions for each of the following categories listed for the novel and the play.)

2. Author's theme and purpose — Why has the author chosen to write about this individual? Did the subject initiate the biography? Is the author interested in "cashing in" on the current popularity of the subject?

3. Author's diction

4. Degree of difficulty

5. Audience

6. Tone of the work

7. Fairness to subject — is the biographer fair and objective? If not, are his prejudices apparent?

8. New insights — What new insights does the author present concerning some aspects of the subject's life?

Does he present the subject in a new light? Has he unearthed some hithertofore unknown facts?

9. Sources — What are the sources used by the biographer — letters, diaries, the subject, the subject's family, personal recollections, library research, other documents? How do any of these sources add to the biography's effectiveness?

10. Author's knowledge — How knowledgeable is the biographer about his subject?

11. Development and overall organization

12. Comparison to other books on the same subject

Facts about the book:

1. What are some of the more important events in the subject's life?

2. What are the subject's major contributions?

3. What are the subject's weaknesses? his strengths?

4. What makes the subject worthy to be the subject of a biography?

5. Cite a humorous incident from the subject's life.

6. If it is an autobiography, cite those incidents which reveal the author's attitude towards himself.

7. What are the subject's physical attributes? intellectual? emotional?

8. What are his ideals?

9. What handicaps did he have to overcome, e.g., Helen Keller's blindness and deafness, Roosevelt's polio.

OTHER NON-FICTION WORKS: In addition to biographies and autobiographies, non-fiction works encompass critical writings, collections of essays (see discussion under *Collections*), and general utilitarian literature such as histories, textbooks, encyclopedias, dictionaries, scientific writings, political analyses, and other kinds of factual accounts. Here, moreso than in reviewing any other genre, it is increasingly difficult to separate the facts about the work from your critical observations; the two are truly intertwined. In writing your review, focus primarily on the author's success in achieving his purpose and in communicating with his audience.

Here are some aspects of the work you may discuss:

1. Thesis — What is the author's thesis as revealed in the Preface or as implied in the text? Does he develop that thesis adequately?

2. Organization — Check the Table of Contents, the Preface, the index, chapter headings, and sub-headings. How well has the material been organized? Is the presentation of material too superficial or too detailed? Does he include too much trivia?

3. Level of difficulty — This, of course, must be judged by the intended audience.

4. Audience — Is the work directed to the professional or to the layman? What background is required of the reader?

5. Readability — Is the layout of the book such that it aids the reader? How easy is it to locate specific information? What about type size? Typography?

6. Timeliness — Is the topic timely? What was the date of the latest revision? Does the author take into account the most recent developments or discoveries in the field?

7. Validity and reliability of the contents.

8. Author's qualifications — What qualifies the author to write on the subject? Is he objective or subjective? Does he manipulate facts? Does he overlook information which might be contradictory to his thesis?

In addition to the above, many of the suggestions made for the other genres are applicable here as well. For example, you can compare the work to other works by the same author or to works dealing with the same subject; you can discuss the tone of the work; you can discuss style, diction, development. No matter which of the foregoing aspects you choose to discuss, remember once again that you must adequately substantiate any impression or opinion with specific incidents from the work.

COLLECTIONS: Since it is rare that you will be called upon to review a single short story, essay or poem — these are rarely, if ever, published under separate cover — you will find your reading of these shorter works limited to collections or anthologies. Such collections may be of all one genre, such as a collection of short stories, or of different genres. Furthermore, the collection may be of works written by one author (sometimes compiled by the author personally) or of the works of different authors compiled by an editor. Either way, it should be apparent that you will not be able to discuss each work within the anthology individually; your emphasis will, therefore, be on the collection as a whole.

Each type of collection will require a slightly different emphasis — a discussion of poetry will be different from one dealing with essays — yet reviews of collections all have something in common. Here are some aspects that you may deal with:

1. Type of collection — Are all the selections of the same genre? Are the works by the same author or different authors? Are they from the same literary period? What is the time span covered by the selections?

2. Organization — Although closely related to the above, what is the arrangement of the works? Is the approach thematic? chronological? generic? Is there a common theme in all of the selections (e.g., James Joyce's *The Dubliners*)? Do the selections have to be read in sequence?

3. Prefatory material — Is there a brief note preceding each work? Does the editor supply biographical or other extrinsic information?

4. Textual notes and explanatory notes — Does the editor supply sufficient notes? Do these notes add to or detract from the collection's effectiveness?

5. Preface — Does the preface give an adequate clue as to the collection's intent?

6. Purpose — What is the editor's or compiler's purpose? How well is that purpose achieved?

7. Appendix — Are there any appendixes? What do they contain? Are they necessary?

8. Audience — What is the intended audience? How effective is the work in reaching that audience? What is the level of difficulty of the selections?

9. Quality — Is there uniformity of quality in the selections? Should some of the selections have been omitted? Some added?

10. Comparison with other anthologies

11. Choose representative selections and discuss these in relation to any of the above.

One final reminder: Do not concentrate so heavily on one selection from the anthology that you — and your reader — lose sight that you are reviewing an entire collection. One selection will not determine the book's worth. On the other hand, do not fail to discuss some of the selections so that you convince your reader that you have read the anthology and not just looked at the book's organization. One way or the other, be certain that you give adequate substantiation from the work to back up any expression of opinion.

SAMPLE REVIEWS: On the following pages you will find some sample reviews of the different genres discussed throughout this book. Hopefully, they are of books with which you are familiar for this will aid you in writing your own reviews. If you are not familiar with the work, and if the review is successful, you should be aware of the reviewer's opinion and of what the book is about once you have finished reading. In reading these samples, concentrate on *how* the reviewer presents his thoughts.

Sample review — novel:

The Town. By William Faulkner. New York: Random House, 1957. 368 pages.

By Joe Skinner

The Town is the second book of a trilogy in which William Faulkner traces the rise of the Snopeses, Flem Snopes in particular, a repellent specimen of white trash who has his first triumphs in The Hamlet when he marries the pregnant daughter of Will Varner, the somewhat feudal lord of Frenchman's Bend. In The Town, Flem continues his upward climb in Jefferson through his shrewd business sense but mainly as the result of Mayor de Spain's sexual attachment for Mrs. Snopes. The story, effectively though at times confusingly told through the narrations of Gavin Stevens, Charles Mallison, and V.K. Ratliff, concerns itself with the strongly opposing values of Flem Snopes and Gavin Stevens, the changing values against the entire time-honored traditions of the South.

To Flem Snopes money and power are the dominating values, and there is absolutely nothing he will not do to achieve these. He uses every means at his disposal, from stealing brass fittings as superintendent of the power plant to using the obvious physical charms of his wife to further his aims. But Faulkner makes it very apparent that the values of Flem are to be disdained, for the old values of the South, the values which Faulkner cherishes, do not exist for Flem. Marriage for love, the sanctity of the home, fairness, honesty, loyalty to one's benefactors, morality, all these Flem discarded for his one overpowering value, the lust for power. As a result, he was able to marry Eula Varner without any thought of love; to pit one power plant employee against the other to enable him to steal the brass, without any thought of fairness or honesty; to use Will Varner for his own purposes without any thought of loyalty; to permit Mayor de Spain to have an affair with Eula without any thought of the sanctity of the home or of the moral values involved. For Flem Snopes there was only one value, power; nothing else mattered.

Pitted against him we have Faulkner's spokesman, the intellectual Phi Beta Kappa, Harvard and Heidelberg educated lawyer of Yoknapatawpha County, Gavin Stevens, the old-fashioned champion of decency and honor, who with his gritty common sense and shrewd insight into poor white philosophy represents the conscience

- 2 -

of Jefferson, and whose code demands that he defend all the values held dear by the South - - and to an extent of the rest of our society - - as well as save Jefferson's good name from being soiled by the Snopeses. But Faulkner lets us know that living up to this code is no easy task, for Lawyer Stevens almost falls prey to that which Flem Snopes represents. Gavin has fallen for the voluptuous charms of Eula Snopes. However, when she comes to his office one night to offer herself to him in return for a favor, it is only his strong moral character and his stronger desire to rid Jefferson of Snopeses that saves him.

It is Gavin Stevens who must maintain his values, the values of Faulkner and the South, and defend them against all the Snopeses, whether it be I.Q. Snopes who ties his mules to a curve in the railroad tracks so he can collect the insurance money, Montgomery Ward Snopes who runs one of the most profitable businesses in Jefferson, showing pornographic pictures, or any of the other innumerable members of the Snopes clan; but it is against Flem Snopes that Stevens must really defend the South. It is Flem's lust for respectability that Faulkner finds most detestable, even more so than the lust for money and power. The Snopeses are symbolic, for both Stevens and Faulkner fear that they will shatter and alter not only the established economic and moral order, but will undermine the entire social structure of the South, for what can be worse than for white trash like Flem Snopes to become respectable?

There is a conflict of values throughout the novel, for all the characters are symbolic; moral and ethical issues are constant and the characters learn and change and suffer whether it be Gavin Stevens, Will Varner, Eula, or the Snopeses. But the main crisis is whether Jefferson and the South - - even the world for that matter - - will be saved from the Flem Snopeses. And although at the end of the book the town has not been rid of them, there is hope, for Flem is sexually impotent. This weakness, coupled with Stevens' successful rescue of Eula's illegitimate daughter, symbolizes that at least some part of the future can be saved from the evil that Flem represents. William Faulkner feels that the possibility of salvation exists, but whether the Gavin Stevenses will continue to rise to the challenge remains to be seen.

Sample review – – play:

"Margaret Fleming." By James A. Herne. In Representative American Plays, from 1767 to the Present Day, edited by Arthur Hobson Quinn. New York: Appleton-Century-Crofts, Inc., 1953. Pages 519–544.

By Jeanine Wasser

Margaret Fleming, a play dealing with the great moral problem of infidelity, was not too favorably received by its critics. Edward A. Dithmar, writing in the December 10, 1891 edition of the New York Times, rather succinctly expressed the consensus of his contemporaries by stating that James A. Herne's play was the " . . . quintessence of the commonplace. Its language is the colloquial English of the shops and streets and the kitchen fire-place. Its personages are the every-day non-entities that some folks like to forget when they go to the theatre . . . The life it portrays is sordid and mean, and its effect upon a sensitive mind is depressing . . . The stage would be a stupid and useless thing if such plays as Margaret Fleming were to prevail . . . [for] love is a mean thing in his play." [1] But how wrong Dithmar and his fellow critics were! Herne's play is a distinguished example of a sociological drama, and its simplicity and sincerity, as well as its characters – – characters who are not types but individuals, real people – – make Margaret Fleming one of the outstanding plays of that era. It was a far cry from the earlier melodrama. Realism in the theater had finally become a reality.

Herne's play is notable for its absence of great theatricals; rather it has that simple, kindly, homey touch which he felt could best reflect true character. The characters are real; they are alive; they grow and develop naturally. Philip, Margaret's unfaithful husband, is drawn with great skill: he is not a mere sensualist or a weakling but a man who has no difficulty distinguishing between his real love for his wife and his sensuous love for Lena. From Lena's death note we learn that he has never even tried to deceive her into believing he loves her. Margaret is a " . . . revelation of the nobility inherent in the cultivated American gentlewoman." [2] She rises to the challenge of her husband's unfaith-

---

[1] Edward A. Dithmar, New York Times, Dec. 10, 1891, in Montrose J. Moses and John M. Brown (eds.), The American Theatre As Seen by Its Critics, 1752–1934 (New York, 1934), p. 143.

[2] Arthur Hobson Quinn, A History of the American Drama from the Civil War to the Present Day, rev. ed. (New York, 1937), I, 141.

- 2 -

fulness, and both her actions and reactions always seem natural and true-to-life.

Even though Dithmar did not think it a virtue, he had to admit the play " . . . is consistent; it is realistic in everything. We see human beings as they are. There are no soliloquies. The meditations of the characters are not spoken aloud. The author has steered clear of all the old conventions of the drama."[3] Dithmar and other critics, as well as the public, condemned Margaret Fleming for the same reason that we find it so commendable - - its strong realism and its lack of forcible dramatic situations and old-fashioned stirring climaxes.

In the scene where Margaret, after learning of Philip's unfaithfulness, starts to nurse the baby boy, Herne revealed the strength of that dramatic action in which, while few or no words are spoken, the relations of human beings are developed or revealed with "the fatal swiftness which is the essential quality of great dramatic moments. The essence of such action is quiet natural expression through word, gesture, or that repose which becomes in itself active . . . It differs radically from the intense brief sentences of melodrama in which the object is not revelation of characters but intensification of situation."[4]

The final scene is perhaps the best. Philip returns to his wife after attempting suicide and is received by Margaret with forgiveness but with an indication that she cannot again be his wife. It is here that she has been bringing up both Lucy and Lena's sons who are playing in the garden. In this scene, Herne leaves us with the feeling of hope that the future can become a little brighter although Margaret and Philip will never regain their original happiness. However, Philip's buoyant steps into the garden are symbolic of hope.

From our modern day vantage point, it is very apparent that Herne's Margaret Fleming made an outstanding contribution to realism in the theater and was, perhaps, instrumental in changing the direction of the American theater. His simplicity and sincerity and his effective, realistic portrayals of his characters make this a truly fascinating play to read. Too bad no one has thought to produce it lately.

---

[3]Dithmar, op. cit., p. 143.

[4]Quinn, op. cit., p. 144.

Sample review - - collection:

Soul on Ice. By Eldridge Cleaver. New York: Dell Publishing Company, 1968.
210 pages.

By Wanda Klugman

Regardless of how one views Eldridge Cleaver - - and it is much easier to view him more dispassionately now than at the time the book was published - - his Soul on Ice is a forceful, gripping, often irritating work. Cleaver, the ghetto-born-and-bred youth, the imprisoned rapist, the Black Panther Minister of Information, speaks his mind in a very literary yet often earthy manner. The collection of letters and essays, written during Cleaver's stay in Folsom Prison, reveal not only his discovery of his blackness but present us - - especially the white society - - with many truisms and observations that we might prefer to remain undisturbed.

Cleaver manages to bring into sharp focus the daily irritations experienced by the Black man in a white society, irritations which are symptomatic. This is perhaps most clearly expressed through a minor incident he recounts in "A Day in Folsom Prison" where he discusses the relationship between the races. Although the races do not fraternize in comfort, Cleaver has found something in common with a "Jewish stud out of New York who fell out of Frisco" (p. 46); they enjoy rapping about the current scene and exchanging reading material. One day, while standing on lunch line and talking, Cleaver notices how increasingly nervous and leery "this cat" is becoming, when he says that he "just remembered" that he had to talk to someone and "splits." Cleaver immediately realizes that Harry Golden's concept of vertical integration and horizontal segregation is taking effect. It is all right to talk to a Black man, but sitting down to eat with him is another matter. Equally as frustrating is the attitude of the guards who tear up Cleaver's pin-ups of white girls and tell him that he can get himself " . . . a colored girl for a pinup [but] - - no white women . . . " (p. 8). Such incidents and observations are sprinkled liberally throughout, heightening our awareness of what it is like to be Black.

Throughout the book Cleaver ranges far and wide, covering a variety of topics, but the reader is always aware that this is Cleaver speaking. He presents us with his commentary on current situations - - the youth rebellion, the Free Speech Movement, the assas-

- 2 -

sination of Malcolm X, the Watts riots, Viet Nam (many of these overshadowed today by more current national and international events); he presents us with his views of the role of the Negro celebrity in American society, the role of boxing as the virility symbol of the American masses and why they reject fighters like Muhammad Ali, and with his views on the Black writer, particularly James Baldwin. Most fascinating perhaps are his views on the relationship of the sexes and the races expressed in the section "White Woman, Black Man." It is here that Cleaver creates his Supermasculine Menial and the Ultrafeminine Doll; it is here that he propounds his philosophy of the "primeval mitosis," the split between the white administrative "mind" and the Black "body," the "Brute Power" function of the Supermasculine Menial." Whether one agrees with his views or not, the ideas are presented clearly, logically, and forcefully.

No matter what Cleaver says in these essays and letters - - and they do not have to be read in sequence - - he says well. His command of the English language is especially commendable in light of his limited formal education and in the realization that he is self-educated. He expresses himself almost lyrically when he discusses his craving for "womanfood" " . . . to look into her eyes, to sniff her primeval fragrance, to hear - - with slaughtered ears - - the sensuous rustling of frivolous garments as legs are crossed and uncrossed beneath a table, to feel the delicate, shy weight of her hand in his . . . " (pp. 23-24). Or when he discusses his desire to be part of the revolutionary movements: " . . . how I'd just love to be in Berkeley right now, to roll in that mud, frolic in that sty of funky revolution to breathe its heady fumes, and look with roving eyes for a new John Brown, Eugene Debs, a blacker-meaner-keener Malcolm X, a Robert Franklin Williams with less rabbit in his hot blood, an American Lenin, Fidel, a Mao-Mao, A MAO MAO, A MAO MAO, A MAO MAO, A MAO MAO . . . " (p. 19). Regardless of his philosophy, Cleaver is extremely easy and delightful to read.

Although Soul on Ice is not as soul-jarring as it was a mere few years ago, Cleaver still manages to illumine areas which we may prefer to keep dark. He speaks his mind, presenting his ideas forcefully, clearly, coherently, and often irritatingly. But they are ideas well-worth reading. One may agree with him or violently disagree with him, but one cannot remain passive. Soul on Ice is the kind of book that grabs the reader by the lapels and makes him want to keep reading. It is a must on everyone's reading list.

John Paul Jones, A Sailor's Biography. By Samuel Eliot Morison. Boston: Little, Brown and Company, 1959. 453 pages.

By Tyrone Starker

If anyone is qualified to write a definitive biography of a sailor, it is surely Samuel Eliot Morison. He is not only a former rear admiral in the United States Navy, but also Professor Emeritus of American History at Harvard, a meticulous researcher, an extensive writer of historical works, and a writer who manages to present historical data more in the style of the novelist than of the historian. Professor Morison has managed to combine all these attributes in the Book-of-the-Month Club selection, John Paul Jones, A Sailor's Biography.

Morison is eminently qualified to write a biography of John Paul Jones. Besides his many years of naval experience, giving him the necessary insights into and an understanding of the sea and of naval warfare, he sailed the English, French, and American waters where Captain Jones had sailed. But this was only in partial preparation for this biography. He also researched thoroughly the American, British, French and Russian naval archives of Paris and the old St. Petersburg. These preparations coupled with the author's known scholarship through such works as the multi-volumed History of United States Naval Operations in World War II, The Maritime History of Massachusetts, The Ropemakers of Plymouth, By Land and by Sea, and his Pulitzer Prize winning Admiral of the Ocean Sea (a biography of Columbus) should readily convince any prospective reader of John Paul Jones that he will be reading the most authoritative account of Jones available to him.

In his own unique, easy-to-read style, Admiral Morison not only reveals many hithertofore little known details about Jones' life, but focuses on the many contradictions and paradoxes within Jones. He tells us, for example, that Jones wrote many times that he had " . . . drawn his sword from pure love of liberty as a 'citizen of the world,' " (p. 3) yet his final service was to the greatest despot of Europe, Catherine of Russia. Furthermore, he claimed contempt for rank, yet he was happiest as le Chevalier Paul Jones at the

- 1 -

- 2 -

Parisian court. And although he pretended to disdain fame, he took every opportunity to make himself known, so that today the name of John Paul Jones is known to practically every school boy, but few know the names of his naval contemporaries.

Morison's account of Jones' life is no dull, dry presentation of facts and data in the style of the scholarly dissertation. Rather it is written in Morison's stimulating prose interspersed with appropriate quotations from letters and from official records. The over-all effect of the book is further heightened through the inclusion of charts and diagrams (making naval maneuvers more comprehendable to the layman) and pictures and illustrations, one of the more interesting ones being Jones as seen by his friends and his enemies (pp. 232-233).

If you have avoided reading biographies of historical figures because you feared they would be dull reading, Morison's John Paul Jones will put those fears to rest. He has managed to capture the essence of an era and the essence of a legendary figure and presented them authoritatively and fascinatingly. You will find that once you have completed this biography, you will anxiously look forward to reading Admiral Morison's other books about the sea and its heroes.

NOTES

APPENDIX

SUGGESTIONS FOR BOOK REPORT TOPICS

In addition to the basic book review-report that has been discussed within this book, there are other approaches to reporting on books that you have read which do not necessarily require criticism nor a personal, subjective response to the work. Such reports are primarily geared to determining whether you have read the work in question and with what depth of understanding. Sometimes these reports can be presented orally.

I. Answer the following questions in well-organized, unified and coherent compositions. Be certain that you cite adequate specific incidents from the work being discussed to substantiate your thesis:

1. In literature we often meet *a character who fascinates us* to the point wnere we would like to meet him in real life. Choose one character from your book and discuss why you would like to meet him.

2. Literature often exposes us to *new places*. Select a place from the book and discuss why you would (or would not) like to visit it.

3. Great literature, if it is truly effective, will give the reader *new insights* and *new experiences*. Discuss what insights or experiences you have gained.

4. Choose any two characters from the book and discuss their *similarities or differences*.

5. The point of view from which a story is told has a distinctive bearing on our attitude towards the events or

characters. Show how the story would be affected if told from the *point of view of another character.*

6. Using the same major events in the story, *rewrite the ending.* Then briefly discuss which ending is more effective.

7. Assume that you are the casting director for a film studio. *Which actor (or actress) would you choose to portray the main character?* Defend your choice.

8. Literature often reflects the *social, political, economic, or religious problems of the period* during which the work is written. Which of these problems are reflected in the work and what is the author's attitude towards them?

9. State *the author's theme,* and then discuss why you agree or disagree with his viewpoint.

10. Authors often make effective use of *symbolism.* Point out some of the symbols the author employed and discuss how they add to the overall effectiveness of the work.

11. We often gain insight into a person's character by how he reacts to certain stimuli. Choose one character and through a discussion of his reaction(s), show *the kind of person he is.*

12. Many books have been sold to the film studios to be made into motion pictures. *Assume that you are in charge of purchasing books for motion pictures.* Discuss why you would consider (or reject) purchasing the book.

II. The following projects can be reported on in writing or orally.

1. You are a door-to-door salesman of books. Give a *sales pitch* for your book.

2. You are the host of a *talk show.* Prepare a list of questions you wish to ask the author.

3. Prepare a *you-are-there script* for one of the scenes from the book.

4. Prepare a short *annotation for a bibliography.*

5. Write a *précis* of the work.

6. Choose three passages from the work which you feel are noteworthy. Tell why you chose each.

7. Prepare a *trial brief* for one of the characters whom you must defend in a court of law.

8. Change the *setting* of the story and discuss how this would affect the story.

9. Set one of the poems to *music*. Discuss why the *musical accompaniment* is apropos.

10. Argue why this book should be limited to certain age groups.

11. Your job is to write blurbs for book jackets. Write the *blurb* for this book.

12. Defend (or reject) the author's choice of a *title*.

13. Make a *time chart* of the major events.

14. Draw a *map* showing the place where the major action takes place.

15. Prepare a *genealogy* chart.

16. Read several *professional reviews* of the book and show why you agree or disagree with their views.

17. Assume you are the author and defend yourself against accusations of *libel*.

18. Assume you are a publisher. Write a *letter to the author* informing him why you have *rejected (or accepted) his manuscript for publication*.

19. Assume that you are the author and you are asked to submit some pertinent *biographical data for publicity*. What information would you supply and why.

20. You are serving on the Pulitzer Prize committee, and you are entitled to *nominate one book*. List your reasons for your choice and prepare to defend your argument.

COPYREADING SYMBOLS

Insert a period:

⊗   He was there ⊗

Insert a comma or semi-colon:

        Therefore, he will ...

Insert apostrophe or quotation marks:

        We'll come.

Capitalize:

≡   Last saturday . . .

Write with lower-case letter:

/   He loves Chemistry.

Abbreviate or spell out:

        Doctor Jones called. . . .

        The 10 men . . . .

Start a new paragraph.

no # **Do NOT start a new paragraph.**

] [**Indent left or right, as indicated.**

Separate letters:

/   Some of our members. . . .

Bring letters together:

        So me of our students. . . .

Delete punctuation mark:

Some, of the boys. . . .

Delete letter, word, or phrase:

Sailling down on the river. . . .

Insert letter, word, or phrase:

Sailing on the river. . . .

Transpose:

Ten men wanted to badly go. . . .

Restore to original text:

Four of the girls. . . .

Set in italics:

The Hamlet is a novel. . . .

Set in boldface type:

Part I must be re-read.

NOTES

NOTES

NOTES

NOTES

NOTES

NOTES